Florida Plants for Wildlife

Florida Plants for Wildlife

A SELECTION GUIDE TO NATIVE TREES AND SHRUBS

Craig N. Huegel

Illustrated by Rani Vajravelu

Florida Native Plant Society
Orlando, Florida

ISBN 1-885258-04-6

Published by
The Florida Native Plant Society
Orders for FNPS books should be addressed to P.O. Box 6116, Spring Hill, FL 34606.

Contents

Acknowledgments _____

This book is dedicated to my parents, Jack and Louise Huegel, who set me on the trail of wild things when I was a young boy, armed only with their patient encouragement, not knowing where the trail might lead, yet confident that I would find my way.

The author thanks those who helped in the production of this publication: Peggy Lantz for encouraging it and for editing and preparing it for publication; Herbert W. Kale, II, for providing a careful review of the manuscript; and numerous members of the Florida Native Plant Society for sharing their time and knowledge.

Preface

Natural Florida is an amazingly diverse and magical place. As urbanization becomes an increasingly familiar backdrop for our lives, many of us feel the need to reestablish some of that naturalness and magic around our homes.

The wise use of native plants can do much to eliminate the monotony and lifelessness of the typical urban setting, but more importantly, native plant landscapes will provide for wildlife, adding a dimension that creates both wonder and excitement. We are called and challenged to take a more eclectic approach to landscaping.

The Florida Native Plant Society hopes that this book will help you choose from Florida's rich diversity of native trees and shrubs to provide food and cover for wildlife where you live and work. No plant is totally devoid of wildlife value, but some are clearly better than others. Your planting choices will have a profound influence on the types of animals that live near you, so you will want to make informed decisions to make your gardening efforts most effective.

The trees and shrubs included in this book were selected because they provide both food (e.g., nuts, seeds, fruit) and cover for animals. Our goal is to increase your appreciation of the many landscaping choices available to you. Use it to help restore habitat for the native wildlife so frequently lost to us in the typical urban landscape.

Planning Your Wildlife Landscape _____ ONE

Florida's rich heritage of native wildlife has evolved to exist in association with native plant communities. Most animals retreat from human-altered landscapes where the focus traditionally has been on aesthetics. That is why, even as this book is being written, 44 percent of Florida's 668 resident vertebrate species are declining. A total of 146 of these currently are listed as endangered, threatened, or species of special concern. Without doubt, the total will increase. Habitat loss is the underlying cause.

The issue in Florida is not loss of animals, but loss of species diversity. Certain native species such as raccoons and opossums have benefited from urbanization, and a great variety of non-native species such as pigeons, starlings, and Old World rats and mice have been introduced into this new and altered landscape and have prospered. What we *are* losing are the many native species dependent on native plant communities not normally preserved in urban developments. Our challenge then is to incorporate elements of native plant communities into the landscapes where we live. Native plants and diversity of wildlife are intertwined.

The Importance of Habitat

You can attract animals with a feeder, but they will not be able to live in that area unless you've also provided for their other needs. This is the essential difference between attracting wildlife and creating habitat. Attracting animals requires someplace else to produce and shelter them. Providing habitat produces wildlife and ensures that the animals will survive over time. You become a wildlife producer instead of merely a wildlife consumer.

Animals live only where their habitat occurs, because this provides them with the food, water, and cover that they need to survive and reproduce. The complicating factor is that each animal has its own specific habitat requirements. Thus, no place provides habitat for every species, and altering a landscape will alter the types and numbers of animals that will live there. Scrub jays are replaced by blue jays when scrublands are replaced by developments dominated by live and laurel oaks. Gray squirrels replace fox squirrels, and Cuban anoles take the place of skinks and racerunners in the typical urban setting.

Providing habitat requires first that you decide which wildlife you can adequately provide for, and then that you understand their habitat needs. A certain amount of planning is involved to be most sucessful. Without it, your results may very well be disappointing, especially if the amount of land that you have to work with is small and the degree of surrounding urbanization is large.

Work within the environmental constraints that you are given. If your landscape is to be a home for wildlife, use plant materials that are appropriate to the growing conditions on your site. If your habitat relies on plants that are not adapted to the normal range of conditions found on the property, it is not properly designed. Your habitat will naturally develop and change over time, but it shouldn't be designed with a high risk of failure.

Providing Wildlife Cover in the Landscape

Cover serves to hide and shelter animals during their daily activities, protects them from the notice and attack of predators, and creates conditions that will enhance their ability to reproduce and raise offspring. All plants have some cover value, but each has different characteristics. If you wish to provide cover for a diversity of animals, it will be necessary for you to use a variety of plants. Too much of any one thing will limit your success.

Plants possess many characteristics that will influence their cover value. Leaf type, for example, can be important. Plants that are evergreen can shelter animals year-round and protect them from cold winter weather. Deciduous plants may have many other uses for wildlife, but they are poor winter cover. Good wildlife landscapes will have at least some areas reserved for evergreen plantings.

Plants with thorns often are exceedingly valuable because they protect nesting birds and other animals from predators. Use them selectively in out-of-the-way places and buffer them with "friendlier" plants in the foreground.

Branch strength and foliage density also should be considered. Few animals choose to nest or hide in plants that do not provide adequate support or concealment. Of course, some plants may provide one, but not the other. Plants can have dense foliage that creates good hiding or escape cover, but have thin branches that offer little support for nesting. Both types of cover need to be considered. Foliage density can be increased by grouping plants together, but branch strength is a factor of the individual plant.

A significant amount of cover also can be provided by dead trees. Many wildlife species depend on cavities in dead limbs and trunks for nesting and escape cover. Primary cavity nesters such as woodpeckers create their own holes, while a large host of secondary users, including bluebirds, chickadees, nuthatches, screech owls, flying squirrels, and rat snakes require cavities created by other wildlife or by natural events. Although the scope of this book is restricted to the use of living plantings, you should never underestimate the value of dead limbs and trees, and they should be left in place wherever they do not pose a safety risk.

One final point about cover is that few animals use only one vertical level within the landscape. Consider cover from the ground to the tree canopy. Large trees, subcanopy trees, and shrubs are equally important. Beneath these, use some type of ground cover or organic mulch. Many wildlife, including a large number of songbirds, spend time on the ground. Do not ignore the importance of cover even at this level.

Additional groundcover for some wildlife can be developed by creating a brush pile. To be useful, brush piles should be open enough that animals can move through the spaces between the materials. Larger limbs, 8 to 10 inches in diameter, will provide for animals such as rabbits, while piles of thinner materials will be used mostly by smaller wildlife.

Providing Wildlife Food in the Landscape

We must critically evaluate our existing landscapes to see how well they provide food for wildlife. Then a plan can be designed to fill in whatever gaps exist.

Insects are an important food source for many animals—birds, mammals, lizards, amphibians and even other insects. Even most seed-eating birds require insects during the nesting season to provide protein for their growing nestlings. Landscaping practices have a great influence on the numbers and types of insects that will be present. Certain flowering plants such as red mulberry (*Morus rubra*) and laurel oak (*Quercus laurifolia*) are excellent at attracting large numbers of pollinating insects when they are in bloom, and these, in turn, will become a feeding station for insect-eating wildlife.

Larval food plants of butterflies and moths also are excellent. Winged maypop (*Passiflora suberosa*), for example, provides food for a variety of passion vine butterfly caterpillars. These caterpillars will serve to feed hungry nestling birds during the spring and summer months. Another important location for insects, worms, and other invertebrates is in organic mulch.

A vast majority of the plants listed in this book have flowers that attract pollinating insects. Some also, such as the pines, have flaky bark that house other types of insect food.

To produce insects for your wildlife, you will need to greatly reduce or eliminate the use of insecticides. Insecticides not only reduce insect availability, but may poison wildlife that consume them shortly after application. By using native plants adapted to your growing conditions, you likely will find that most pest problems will take care of themselves naturally. If you design your landscape to provide wildlife habitat, it should also be in harmony with your local environment. Let natural processes work whenever possible and have faith that they will.

Most of the plants in your landscape will produce food directly through fruits, nuts, and seeds. You will have many plants of this type to choose from, so weigh the relative merits of each possibility carefully.

In a complete habitat, food must be available year-round. If everything ripens over a two-month period, there will be little for wildlife to feed on during the other ten months. Select plants so that their fruiting times will be staggered throughout the year.

Size of the fruit is another important consideration. Large fruit may be impossible for small birds to consume. Even among plant species in the same genus, there may be great differences in fruit size. The variability of acorn sizes within the oaks (*Quercus* spp.) is a good example of this. If small, fruit-eating birds are important to you, select plants that produce fruits that are small enough for them to eat.

Food also varies in terms of taste and palatability. Just as many of us shy away from healthy foods that offend our sense of taste, wildlife may choose certain foods more than others for the same reasons. Generally, foods that taste good to humans also taste good to wildlife. By selecting highly palatable foods, your landscape will get more wildlife use. This does not mean that less palatable foods are undesirable, for the poor-tasting foods will remain available when others have been consumed. In the late winter this is especially important.

A final consideration is the food volume and dependability of your food plants. Some plants, such as beautyberry (*Callicarpa americana*), produce huge quantities of fruit per plant each year. You should use these plants sparingly and save the extra space for different plant species with different wildlife values. Other useful plants, such as some of the oaks, don't produce reliable fruit crops every year. If your landscape plan depends on acorns and you wish to use oaks with this trait, you should incorporate additional oak species to compensate for poor production years.

Food availability also may depend upon the sexual characteristics of the plants. Plants are either monoecious or dioecious. A dioecious plant, such as any of the hollies, is either a male or a female. The male plant pollinates the female plant, and only the female plant produces fruit. In comparison, each monoecious plant has male and female flowers on one plant, or each flower has both male and female parts. Monoecious plants can pollinate themselves, and all individuals bear fruit. In a wildlife landscape, it is important to consider this characteristic. If possible, dioecious species should be sexed prior to planting. This will avoid the problem of having space tied up with males that are not needed for food production. You should probably have no more than one male for every six female plants. When prior sexing is not possible, plant dioecious plants in groups of at least three, and if you end up with a bad mix of sexes, don't be reluctant to replace some of them.

Be sure that your final plant selections are based on the needs of your wildlife. Avoid the temptation to add extraneous species that aren't really contributing. Making tough decisions early will yield great benefits over time.

How To Use This Book _____

Much of our knowledge on the subject of wildlife gardening is in its infancy. Wildlife biologists would have a difficult time assessing the relative importance of each native plant to any given wildlife species in a natural setting. The value of each plant becomes even more obscured when we place them in areas disturbed by urbanization.

The trees and shrubs in this book are native to Florida and have characteristics that make them good providers of both food and cover for wildlife. The information presented is intended to help guide you in assessing their uses within your landscape. Brief descriptions of aesthetic considerations also are included. Some of the plants are uncommon and may be difficult to obtain, but they are included to encourage more widespread use of them in landscaping. All of these factors will play a role in your final landscape decisions.

Plants are arranged alphabetically by families because family characteristics are important in understanding how wildlife use them. Although this may be a bit cumbersome for nontaxonomists, I feel that it will help your understanding in the long run. An index included at the back of this book is designed to assist in locating individual species so that they can be more easily found in the text. Species within each family are alphabetized by scientific name instead of common name, because common names for many of these plants are confusing. Use the index to locate common names and their page location in the text. For species with several widely used common names, I have listed the most commonly used one first, with others following a slash.

The icons alongside each species description make it easy for you to assess quickly whether the plant is suitable for the habitat you are designing.

The shaded portion of the tiny map of Florida indicates the part of Florida in which the plant naturally occurs. Although many native plants can be successfully grown outside their natural range, the best results will occur within the region highlighted on the map.

If you wish to experiment with plants that are not native to your area, be cautious because they may not perform as well as they would in their natural range.

 indicates the plant is a large tree (generally >40 feet at maturity) with a full canopy.

 indicates a small tree (usually <30 feet at maturity).

 indicates a shrub.

 indicates the plant has ornamental value (flowers or leaf color) that may be attractive to humans—as well as insects, hummingbirds, or butterflies.

 indicates the plant provides fleshy fruits.

 indicates the plant provides nuts or seeds.

 indicates that the plant must have wet soil or more moisture than would be provided by ordinary rainfall.

 indicates that the plant must have well-drained soil and a sunny location.

 indicates the plant is a food for butterflies or caterpillars. You should be aware that not all butterflies are large and showy, and that some butterflies have restricted ranges compared to the geographic range where their plants can be grown. You may need additional research if butterflies are a strong interest.

 indicates that the plant is especially attractive to nesting birds.

Plant Descriptions ——————————————— THREE

Aceraceae (Maple family)

This family of woody trees and shrubs is represented in North America only by the maples (*Acer* spp.). In Florida, five species are native. Nearly all are medium- to large-sized (40–90 feet) deciduous trees. Although maples are useful as shade trees, they are not especially important to wildlife. The winged seeds, always produced in the spring, are eaten mostly by squirrels and other rodents. The crowns provide cover for nesting birds and other wildlife. Maples generally grow quickly to maturity, but many of the species are weak and relatively short-lived.

Chalk maple (*Acer leucoderme*) is the rarest and smallest (to 30 feet) maple native to eastern North America. It is found only in scattered locations in north Florida, and inhabits upland alkaline sites along wooded bluffs and ravines. Its leaves are similar to the more common Florida sugar maple (*A. saccharum* var. *floridanum*), but three-lobed leaves are more common than five-lobed ones. Chalk maple gets its name from the white bark of its trunk, and this gives the tree added ornamental value.

Box elder (*A. negundo*) is a short-lived, relatively weak tree native to north and north-central Florida. Although it will grow in a variety of conditions, it does best in moist rich soils. Box elder, sometimes known as ash-leaf maple, has a distinctive broad crown and leaves that are composed of three or five leaflets, much like an ash.

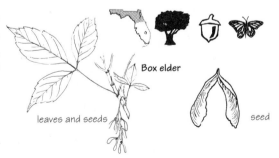

Box elder

leaves and seeds

seed

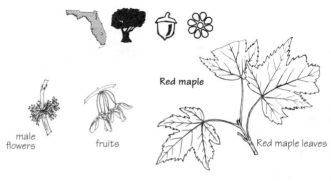

male
flowers

fruits

Red maple

Red maple leaves

Red maple (*A. rubrum*) is the most wide-ranging and commonly used maple in Florida. Although it occurs principally in hardwood wetlands throughout the state, it will grow well in nearly every soil of wet to average moisture. Red maples get their name from the color of their flowers and newly developing seeds in the spring and from the color of their leaves in fall. Some trees are dioecious with the males producing none of the distinctive winged seeds. Red maple leaves are extremely variable in shape and can confuse identification. Florida trees do not need cold temperatures to produce flowers and fruit, but out-of-state stock do and should be avoided, especially in central and south Florida.

Silver maple (*A. saccharinum*) is another fast-growing, short-lived maple that occurs in a few north Florida locations in rich, moist soils. Like the red maple, it is sometimes dioecious. Silver maple is so named because the undersides of its leaves are silvery white and are attractive when the wind blows through them. Leaves also are distinctively five-lobed.

Florida sugar maple (*A. saccharum* var. *floridanum*) is a distinct subspecies of the common sugar maple, which ranges across eastern North America. It generally is smaller than northern sugar maples (about 60 feet at maturity) with smaller, three- or five-lobed leaves, and whitish bark. The leaves turn bright yellow in the fall in north and north-central Florida, eventually turning brown by winter. Unlike other maples, the brown leaves tend to remain on the tree until spring. Florida sugar maples naturally occur in moist upland sites (often in alkaline soils) in north and central Florida. This is the strongest and most long-lived native maple species.

Anacardaceae (Sumac family)

The sumacs are a family of shrubs and small trees represented by many economically important species, such as the mango, cashew, and pistachio in the tropics, and a variety of widespread "weeds" such as the introduced Brazilian pepper ("Florida holly"). Many sumac species produce a milky sap that may be either poisonous or irritating to humans.

Sensitivity to these irritants varies. The three genera of sumacs native to Florida are valuable to wildlife for food. Most are deciduous and provide only limited cover. Native sumacs annually produce large numbers of round, 1/8-inch-diameter fruit.

Poisonwood (*Metopium toxiferum*) is a small (to about 40 feet) tree of south Florida coastal dunes, hardwood hammocks, and disturbed sites. As its name implies, poisonwood produces a highly caustic sap that can cause serious skin and mucous membrane irritations to people who handle any part of it. Therefore, its use in the home landscape is not recommended. Birds and other wildlife, however, are attracted to the many yellowish orange fruit that are produced mostly in late fall, and its evergreen nature provides a good source of cover.

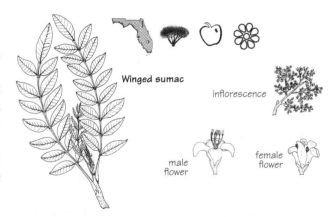

Winged sumac

inflorescence

male flower

female flower

Winged sumac/shiny sumac (*Rhus copallina*) occurs throughout Florida in a wide variety of soils and habitats. Often occurring as a thicket-forming shrub, it may reach 25 feet in height under good growing conditions. This is a fast-growing, short-lived species. Winged sumac flowers in midsummer, and numerous reddish fruits are available by fall to the many songbirds that favor it. Uneaten fruits will persist on the plant well into winter. This shrub does not produce allergic reactions to people, and its brilliant red fall color enhances its value in the landscape. One possible drawback, however, is its tendency to produce suckers, making it difficult to maintain in small areas. The common names are derived from its shiny green leaves and the winglike appendages along the leaf stalks.

Smooth sumac (*Rhus glabra*) is similar in characteristics to winged sumac, but occurs naturally in Florida only in a few Panhandle counties. Smooth sumac differs in general appearance by having leaves with larger leaflets and lacking winged edges along the leaf stalks.

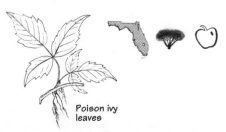

Poison ivy leaves

Poison ivy (*Toxicodendron radicans*) is a familiar component of many natural ecosystems throughout Florida. Although it is often a vine, older specimens can become shrublike. Poison ivy is a useful wildlife plant because it produces large quantities of white berries favored by many birds and small mammals. It is not recommended for home landscapes, however, because all parts of it can cause extreme irritations to human skin and mucous membranes.

Poison oak (*Toxicodendron toxicarium*) shares many of the above characteristics. It differs by its shrublike growth habit, its tendency to spread by underground runners, and by its oaklike leaf shape. This species also occurs throughout Florida.

Poison sumac (*Toxicodendron vernix*) is a small tree that looks much like the sumacs (*Rhus* spp.). Poison sumac has a limited distribution in Florida, occurring in wetlands in north and north-central counties. Its drooping clusters of white berries are favored by many birds, but its use in the home landscape is not recommended because it often causes severe allergic reactions in people.

Annonaceae (Custard-apple family)

This family of trees and shrubs is well-represented throughout Florida in a wide variety of habitats. All produce fleshy edible fruits that are readily eaten by small to medium-sized mammals, such as rodents, opossums, raccoons, and foxes, but are of little use to birds. Some also have fruit that are of limited use to people, but fruit production is often sporadic and undependable. Most members of this family provide little value as wildlife cover.

Pond apple (*Annona glabra*) is a medium-sized (about 40 feet), semideciduous tree native to the edge of freshwater wetlands in south Florida. It has some cold tolerance, but should not be planted much north of Lake Okeechobee. The large, glossy leaves, creamy-white flowers, dense, up-turned branches, and enlarged trunks give this tree character. The 3- to 5-inch, apple-shaped fruits ripen in fall.

PAWPAWS (*Asimina* spp.) are a varied genus with representatives throughout Florida. All produce banana-shaped fruits that are edible, and the tree pawpaw (*A. triloba*) is sometimes planted for its food value. All species also serve as larval food for the zebra swallowtail butterfly.

Flag pawpaw (*Asimina incarna*) is so named because of its large, showy, white flowers. This 4-foot shrub produces many stems from the ground. It is found from north to south-central Florida in well-drained, sandy soils.

Long-leaved pawpaw (*A. longifolia*) is similar to flag pawpaw in growth form, but differs by having long linear leaves. It occurs in north and north-central Florida in well-drained, sandy uplands.

Scrub pawpaw (*A. obovata*) is a robust shrub that may reach 12 feet in height, although it normally is much smaller. Its large, fragrant, showy white flowers give it much landscape value, but it requires very well-drained, sandy soils to survive. This shrub is native from north-central to south Florida and has some salt tolerance.

Scrub pawpaw

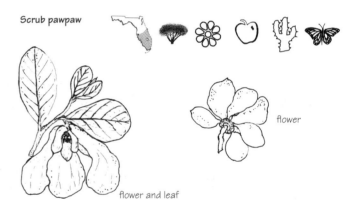

flower

flower and leaf

Small-flowered pawpaw (*A. parviflora*) is a small tree that may reach 18 feet in height. Its small maroon flowers are not showy, and the plant often goes unnoticed. This pawpaw occurs from north to central Florida in the understory of various moist woodlands. It is best grown in similar conditions.

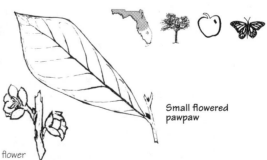

Small flowered pawpaw

flower

Dwarf pawpaw (*A. pygmaea*) is a low-growing, multi-stemmed shrub that rarely exceeds 12 inches in height, making it a useful ground cover. The pinkish white flowers, often with maroon centers, are attractive. Dwarf pawpaw is native in north and central Florida in flatwoods and fields.

Reticulated pawpaw (*A. reticulata*) is a native of poorly drained, sandy soil in central and south Florida. It is a multi-stemmed shrub that can reach about 4 feet in height. The flowers are white and showy. This species is a good choice for areas that periodically flood for brief durations.

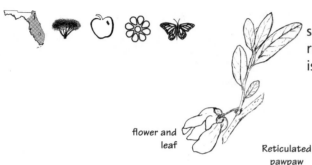

flower and leaf

Reticulated pawpaw

flower

Four-petaled pawpaw (*A. tetramera*) is an exceedingly rare shrub that occurs naturally only in a few well-drained, sandy scrubs in Martin and Palm Beach counties. Its appearance and requirements are similar to those of *A. obovata*, but most flowers have four petals instead of the three seen in other species.

Tree pawpaw/dog banana (*A. triloba*) is an attractive, small, deciduous tree (to about 35 feet) with large green leaves and small maroon flowers. The leaves turn a brilliant yellow in the fall, and there is a small commercial market for the 2- to 3-inch fruit. This attractive tree is native to the Florida Panhandle and is not a good choice for areas farther south. It is shade tolerant and prefers rich, moist soils.

SQUIRREL-BANANAS (*Deeringothamnus* spp.) are a small genus closely related to the pawpaws. They are represented by two species—beautiful squirrel-banana and yellow, or rugel's, squirrel-banana (*D. pulchellus* and *D. rugelii*, respectively), both of which are listed as endangered by the state and federal government. Both also have extremely restricted natural ranges in areas of northeastern Florida. Squirrel-bananas are small (to about 1 foot), multi-stemmed shrubs that prefer poorly drained pine flatwoods soils. The small fruits are similar to those of the pawpaws and likely are used the same way by wildlife. The genus also may serve as a larval food source for the zebra swallowtail butterfly, but research is lacking.

Aquifoliaceae (Holly family)

This family is well-represented in Florida by a variety of deciduous and evergreen trees and shrubs native to a wide diversity of habitats. Hollies are dioecious, but some species will cross-pollinate others. Most produce fruit that are used by many birds and small mammals, and many also provide excellent cover because of their dense foliage and branching structure.

Carolina holly (*Ilex ambiqua*) is a deciduous, shrubby tree that may reach about 15 feet in height. It is adaptable to growing conditions from white sand scrubs to fertile woodlands, but requires good drainage. This is one of my favorite hollies due to its shiny, rich green foliage and bright red, 1/3-inch fruits. Fruits ripen in late summer and will persist well into winter after the leaves fall. It is native from north to south-central Florida.

Sarvis holly (*I. amelanchier*) is the rarest of Florida's native hollies, occurring in isolated populations in the western Panhandle, and generally in moist woodlands. This is a large, deciduous shrub that may reach 15 feet in height. Leaves are dull green and often slightly pubescent, while the 1/3-inch, red fruits are attached to the stems by distinctive stalks.

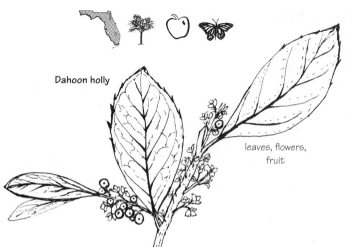

Dahoon holly

leaves, flowers, fruit

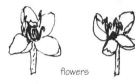

flowers

Dahoon holly (*I. cassine*) is an evergreen tree that may reach 25 feet in height. The leaves are without spiny teeth. Although dahoon holly occurs naturally at the edge of wetlands, it is very adaptable to growing conditions and can even prosper in parking lot medians. It also is Florida's most widely distributed holly, occurring throughout the state, including the Keys. The fruits are very small (1/4 inch) and vary in color from yellowish to red.

Large gallberry/sweet gallberry (*I. coriacea*) is an evergreen, wetland shrub that may reach 15 feet in height. Its 1/3-inch, black fruits are relatively sweet and well used by wildlife. They do not persist on the plant into winter, however. The thin branches provide some hiding cover, but do not offer much support for nesting. Large gallberry is native to the northern half of Florida. Its use should be restricted to moist soils such as the edge of ponds.

Possumhaw holly (*I. decidua*), is a shrubby, deciduous holly native to lowland woods in north and central Florida. It can be a small tree to about 30 feet, but often it is a large shrub. The 1/3-inch fruits are orange-red in color and persist well into winter. This holly often is used outside of Florida, but has received little attention here. It can be a very striking addition to the home landscape, and is adaptable, once established.

often is used outside of Florida, but has received little attention here. It can be a very striking addition to the home landscape, and is adaptable, once established.

Common gallberry (*I. glabra*) is a small (to 8 feet) evergreen shrub common to much of Florida's pine flatwoods and wetland edges, except in extreme southern regions. The shiny green leaves and black fruit give it landscape appeal, but the bitterness of the 1/3-inch fruit greatly reduces its food value. Gallberry's small stature and thin branches offer little cover value. It is most valuable in the understory of plantings in wet or poorly drained soils.

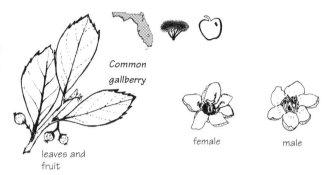

Common gallberry

female   male

leaves and fruit

Tawnyberry holly (*I. krugiana*) is restricted to south Florida—the state's only cold-sensitive holly. This shrubby, evergreen holly may eventually reach 30 feet in height. It is native to a variety of alkaline habitats, but requires some shade to prosper. The black, 1/4-inch fruits ripen in late summer. Prior to that time, they are yellowish red—hence, the common name. Also distinct are the leaves, which are broad with long, pointed tips, resembling somewhat the leaves of some cherries (*Prunus* spp.). Tawnyberry holly has moderate value as hiding cover, but its thin branches provide little nest support.

Myrtle holly (*I. myrtifolia*) is sometimes referred to as myrtle dahoon and is closely related to *I. cassine*. Most often a shrub, myrtle holly may grow to 25 feet. It is native to the northern two-thirds of Florida in wetland areas. A distinctive feature of this holly is its small, narrow, evergreen leaves. This, and its open character, reduces somewhat its value as a cover plant, but its 1/4-inch, orangish red fruits are used by many wildlife.

American holly (*I. opaca*) and its various cultivars and hybrids (e.g., East Palatka and Suwanee holly) is one of the most commonly used native trees. Its relatively slow growth is balanced by its adaptability and long life. True American holly is characterized by spiny, evergreen leaves. This greatly enhances its value as cover to songbirds and other wildlife.

Some forms lack the leaf spines and the protection this affords. American holly is native to the northern two-thirds of Florida in a variety of soil conditions. It will tolerate shade, but its growth form under these conditions will be less dense. Mature heights may reach 45 feet. The 1/3- to 1/2-inch fruits normally are bright red, but yellow forms occur.

Scrub holly (*I. opaca* var. *arenicola*) is either a distinct species or a distinct subspecies of American holly described above. This is a small, compact tree (to about 15 feet) that is confined to well-drained, sandy scrubs of central Florida. It cannot tolerate other soil types and grows best under full sun. The leaves often are greatly curled and spiny, while fruits are orange-red in color and tend to be less succulent than other hollies. Scrub holly is a good food plant and is one of the best cover plants for deep sandy soil.

Winterberry (*I. verticillata*) is a common wetland holly in the eastern United States, but it has a limited distribution in Florida, occurring only in northern areas of the Panhandle. Therefore, it has limited uses in the state. This is a deciduous, multi-stemmed shrub that may reach 20 feet in height. Winterberry is perhaps most distinctive in the winter months when the dark bark of the stems and the many 1/4-inch, bright red fruits become most noticeable.

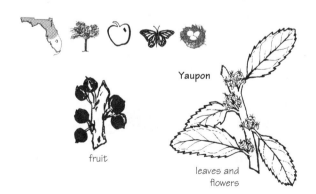

Yaupon

fruit

leaves and
flowers

Yaupon (*I. vomitoria*) is one of the most adaptable of all Florida's native hollies and one of the best wildlife plants available. This multi-trunked shrub eventually will reach 25 to 30 feet in height and then becomes tree-like. The dense branching pattern and dark evergreen leaves provide excellent cover for songbirds and other wildlife, while the many 1/4-inch, shiny red fruits serve as an important food source. Yaupon responds well to shearing and thus makes an excellent hedge or thicket. The whitish bark adds to its beauty. Yaupon occurs naturally from north to south-central Florida in a variety of upland and floodplain habitats. It also grows in coastal dunes and is quite salt tolerant. The leaves contain caffeine and make an excellent tea, despite its scientific name.

Araliaceae (Ginseng family)

This family includes ginseng, widely known for its medicinal root, and the ivies, among others. Aralias produce many small, round, fleshy fruits which are used by many species of wildlife. Only one woody species is native to Florida.

Devil's walking stick/Hercules club (*Aralia spinosa*) is so named because the trunk, branches, and even the leaf stems are armed abundantly with stiff sharp spines. There-fore, its use should be limited to those areas where this would not be a problem. Devil's walking stick is a small deciduous tree (to about 20 feet) that occurs mostly in moist, fer-tile, well-drained woodlands in north and central Florida. It grows rapidly, but is short-lived, and does best in a partly shady area. This tree can provide an interesting and at-tractive accent in the landscape. Its twice-compound leaves can be 3 to 4 feet long and nearly as wide. Leaves occur only at the crown. White flowers cover the crown in summer well after the leaves appear, and the dark purple, 1/8-inch fruits are ripe by fall. Devil's walking stick will sucker, if allowed to, and form a thicket. Single specimens provide little cover for wildlife, but thickets provide good escape cover. The fruits are used by many birds and small mammals.

Betulaceae (Birch family)

Members of this family are deciduous trees or shrubs, and in general they are more widely distributed in regions north of Florida. Hazelnuts (*Corylus* spp.) are important wildlife plants, but are not represented in this state. Birches (*Betula*) and alders (*Alnus*) have sig-nificant wildlife value in more northern states, but the two species, one in each genus, na-tive to Florida are not especially useful except as cover. The two species described here have greater wildlife use.

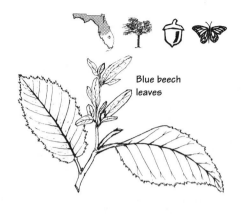

Blue beech leaves

Blue beech/American hornbeam, musclewood, ironwood (*Carpinus caroliniana*) is a small (to 30 feet), understory tree that occurs naturally in moist woodlands in north and central Florida. Because of its shade tolerance, it may be used beneath taller canopy trees. Blue beech has an attractive blue-gray, "muscled" trunk and wide-spreading branches. This tree provides fairly good nesting cover in its branches, but the 1/3-inch nutlets, which ripen in the fall, are of minor use to birds and small mammals. Also, good seed crops are produced only every three to five years.

Eastern hop hornbeam (*Ostrya virginiana*) is another small tree (to about 40 feet) common to woodland understories. Its distribution in Florida, however, does not extend south beyond north-central Florida. Its outer bark develops thin strips that peel away from the trunk. Hop hornbeam gets its name from the fruiting structures that look like the hops used in beer production. The 1/4-inch nutlets inside have limited use to some birds and small mammals. They ripen in the fall, but often persist on the trees until winter. Hop hornbeam provides good nesting and hiding cover.

Boraginaceae (Borage family)

This moderately large family includes some commonly grown herbs and wildflowers, such as borage, forget-me-nots, and heliotrope. Only two genera of trees and shrubs in Florida have much value for wildlife food and cover, and they are native only to south Florida because of their lack of cold tolerance.

STRONGBARKS (*Bourreria* spp.) are notable for their many clusters of white flowers in the summer that attract butterflies, and their large numbers of round, 1/2-inch, orange-red fruits that ripen in the fall and feeds many birds and small mammals. They are evergreen with 1-inch to 3-inch, oval leaves, relatively dense branches, and rapid growth. Strongbarks are tolerant of alkaline soils and can be grown in partial shade at the edge of woodland plantings.

Smooth strongbark (*Bourreria cassinifolia*) is known from only two localities in Florida. It is a multi-branched shrub that does not exceed 7 feet in height.

Bahama strongbark (*B. ovata*) is a shrubby tree that may reach 30 feet in height. This species has the widest natural distribution in south Florida and is common in many areas of the Keys.

Rough strongbark (*B. radula*) is very rare in Florida and may now be extirpated outside of cultivation. It is very similar to Bahama strongbark (*B. ovata*), but its leaves are densely hairy and the fruits are somewhat larger.

Bloodberry/butterfly bush (*Cordia globosa*) is a weakly branched, evergreen shrub that rarely exceeds 8 feet in height. It is native to south Florida and the Keys and is usually found in upland hammock sites. The 1/4-inch white flowers that appear in small clusters at the branch tips during most months are attractive to butterflies and other insects. The 1/8-inch bright red fruits ripen several months later and are eaten primarily by birds. Bloodberry is adaptable to a variety of conditions in frost-free landscape settings and is a useful food source. Its many branches provide some escape cover, especially if planted in a grouping, but its weak branches are not useful for nesting.

Geiger tree (*C. sebestena*) is a widely planted ornamental tree throughout south Florida, but it is native only to the southernmost Keys. This small (to 20 feet), evergreen tree is characterized by a dense, rounded crown and broad, oval, dark green leaves. Its most noticeable feature, however, is the clusters of 1- to 1 1/2-inch-wide, bright orange, trumpet-shaped flowers that bloom nearly year-round. Besides their outstanding aesthetic value, these blooms attract hummingbirds and a wide variety of insect pollinators. The white, 1- to 1 1/2-inch fruits ripen several months later. Each fruit consists of a thin, sweet, fleshy

exterior surrounding one or two seeds. These are mostly used by mammals. Geiger tree has moderate value as wildlife cover, but its food value is somewhat restricted.

Burseraceae (Gumbo-limbo family)

This family is represented by only one species in Florida.

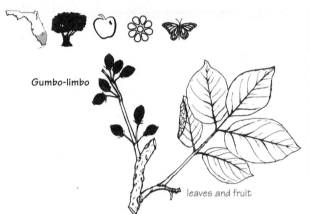

Gumbo-limbo

leaves and fruit

Gumbo-limbo (*Bursera simaruba*) is a widespread south Florida tree that is tolerant of a variety of growing conditions, including salt spray. It may exceed 60 feet in height and grows rapidly. Its compound leaves are deciduous for a brief period in early winter at the time its small white flowers appear. The 1/2-inch, reddish fruits ripen in about a year and are of moderate value to birds and small mammals. The broad canopy provides some cover. Gumbo-limbo is most notable for its distinctive, shiny reddish brown bark that scales away from the trunk in large sheets. It also is extremely easy to propagate. Even large branches will root and form new trees when simply shoved into moist sand and left alone.

Canellaceae (Wild cinnamon family)

This is a small family of tropical evergreen trees with one member native to extreme south Florida.

Cinnamon bark (*Canella winterana*) is a small (to 30 feet) tree that occurs primarily in coastal woodlands. As its name implies, the bark smells like cinnamon when bruised. The dense, rounded crown of this tree and its rather large, thick, aromatic leaves give it good value as wildlife cover. The small clusters of 1/2-inch, round, bright red fruits ripen in winter, but often persist on the trees until early spring. They are eaten by a variety of birds and small mammals. This beautiful small tree has much potential for south Florida land-scapes in both sunny and partly shady areas.

Caprifoliaceae (Honeysuckle family)

This family is composed primarily of shrubs and vines distributed mostly in temperate regions. Many plants have great ornamental and wildlife value, and some are commonly grown in cultivation. All Florida species discussed here have broad heads (umbels) of white flowers followed by masses of succulent fruit that are especially attractive to birds.

Elderberry (*Sambucus canadensis*, syn. *S. simpsonii*) is an extremely common shrub or small tree in wet and moist soil habitats and in disturbed areas throughout Florida. It will tolerate nearly every type of growing condition. Although single specimens have little cover value, elderberries will sucker to form thickets of good cover if left alone. Flowering and fruit production will occur throughout the year, and the vast quantities of 1/5-inch, edible, dark purple fruit are attractive to many birds and mammals. In north Florida, elderberry is a deciduous shrub, but in south Florida it is evergreen and often forms a small tree (to 20 feet) with a rounded crown.

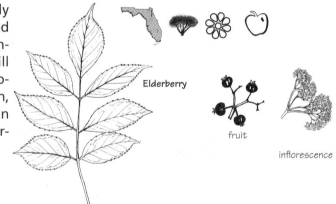

Elderberry

fruit

inflorescence

VIBURNUMS (*Viburnum* spp.) are a genus of deciduous shrubs with opposite leaves. Five species are native to Florida. As a rule, viburnums are native to mixed woodland plant communities and they prefer fertile, moist soils. In cultivation, however, most are quite adaptable and tolerate a range of soil and light conditions. Showy white clusters of flowers appear in the spring, and the 1/4- to 1/3-inch, purplish fruits ripen by late summer.

Maple-leaved viburnum (*Viburnum acerifolium*) is a slender, multi-stemmed shrub that rarely exceeds 6 feet in height. Its three-lobed leaves look similar to those of the red maple—hence, its name. These leaves turn a rich red color in the fall. This shrub is common in northern woodlands into Canada, but is limited in Florida to well-drained woodland soils in the Panhandle. Used within its natural range, maple-leaved viburnum is especially useful in a naturalized woodland landscape where a shade-tolerant understory shrub is desired. Because it spreads by underground runners, it eventually will form colonies if left alone.

Southern arrow-wood (*V. dentatum*) is another multi-stemmed shrub whose natural range is restricted to north Florida. Unlike the maple-leaved viburnum, however, it is a highly variable species and adaptable to a broader range of growing conditions. I have seen it used successfully in several south-central Florida landscapes. Southern arrow-wood gets its name from its abundant arrow-straight stems. The leaves are large with sharply toothed margins. Greenish white flowers are followed by numerous attractive, blue-black fruit. This 6- to 10-foot shrub can be used in moist to average soils and in full sun to partly shady locations.

Possumhaw viburnum (*V. nudum*) is a large shrub that may reach 15 feet in height. It occurs in wet to moist soils in north to north-central Florida, but can adapt to average soils when grown in cultivation. Possumhaw has simple, oval-shaped leaves. This is a relatively open shrub with a broad, rounded crown. Although it does not excel as a source of wildlife cover, its large flower heads produce abundant crops of dark purple fruit.

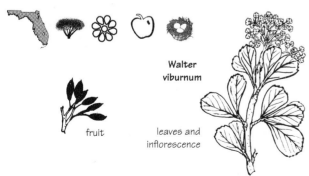

Walter
viburnum

fruit

leaves and
inflorescence

Walter viburnum (*V. obovatum*) is the most adaptable and widely distributed viburnum in the state. This densely branched, shrubby tree, which may reach 30 feet in height, occurs in a variety of moist soil habitats from the central Panhandle to parts of south Florida. Although many references describe this viburnum as an evergreen, it loses most or all of its small, dark green leaves for a brief period in the winter. Nevertheless, it is one of the best shrubs for providing wildlife cover. Walter viburnum has smaller flower heads (cymes) than Florida's other native species, but the sheer number of them in the early spring makes this shrub quite stunning. The flattened, elliptical fruits, ripening from red to black, are available in early fall. Walter viburnum naturally occurs in moist forest soil habitats, but it is extremely adaptable and quite drought tolerant once established. Specimens grown in shady locations will be more lanky than those in full sun. It also responds well to shearing and makes a nice hedge. If allowed to, Walter viburnum will spread by underground suckers and create a thicket.

Rusty viburnum/southern blackhaw (*V. rufidulum*) is a shrub or shrubby tree that may reach 20 feet in height. Its preferred habitats are fertile, well-drained soils and it occurs naturally in north and north-central Florida. It has good tolerance for alkaline soils, also. Rusty viburnum has rounded, 2- to 3-inch, slightly toothed leaves that are so glossy that they look almost wet. In the fall, they turn a variety of hues including red, purple, orange, and yellow. Flower heads are scattered across the plant in loose clusters and appear after the leaves have developed in late spring. These are followed by large, purplish black fruits in the fall. This is a beautiful shrub for partly shady areas within a naturalized woodland landscape.

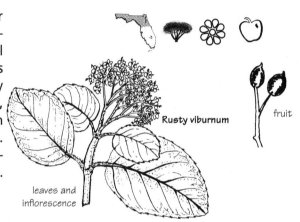

Rusty viburnum

fruit

leaves and
inflorescence

Celastraceae (Bittersweet family)

This family in Florida is composed of shrubs and small trees with opposite leaves. Five genera are native here, four of which are found only in south Florida. The flowers generally are small and inconspicuous. Fruits are capsules or berrylike with a hard inner seed or a seed surrounded by a thin fleshy covering (i.e., an aril), and are designed to be eaten and dispersed by birds.

Rhacoma (*Crossopetalum rhacoma*) is an evergreen, shrubby tree that may reach 20 feet, but is usually much smaller. This is primarily a tropical species; in Florida it is confined to the Keys, only rarely occurring on the southern mainland. Rhacoma is good at providing cover, but because its branches are slender and weak, it is not important for most nesting wildlife. The small, reddish flowers and the 1/4-inch, bright red fruits are produced nearly year-round. This plant occurs naturally in a variety of habitats and tolerates a range of light and soil conditions. It also is salt tolerant.

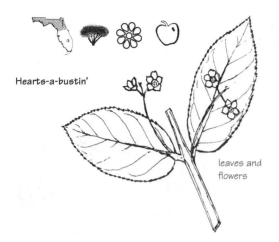

Hearts-a-bustin'

leaves and flowers

Hearts-a-bustin'/strawberry bush (*Euonymus americanus*) is a weakly branched, open, deciduous shrub that rarely exceeds 6 feet in height. It is native to woodland habitats in north and central Florida, usually in the forest understory. This shrub will tolerate temporary flooding and prefers at least partial shade. The leaves turn an attractive red in the fall. Hearts-a-bustin' is so named because its 1-inch, red fruits burst open in the fall, exposing up to five scarlet arils inside. Despite the landscape value that this shrub provides when clumped in the proper location, its seeds have only limited food value and its structure offers little wildlife cover.

False boxwood (*Gyminda latifolia*) is a large tropical evergreen shrub (to 20 feet) that occurs naturally in Florida in coastal hammocks and scrubs in extreme south Florida and the Keys. The light-green oval leaves are 1 to 2 inches long and are dense enough on the thin, reddish brown branches to provide some cover. The 1/4-inch, purplish black fruits are eaten by birds and some mammals. False boxwood is dioecious, so only female plants will provide fruit. Flowering and fruiting occur in all months except winter.

Florida mayten (*Maytenus phyllanthoides*) is a very densely leaved, 20-foot shrub that is native to coastal south Florida. It is evergreen and very salt tolerant. Because of its growth form, mayten provides excellent hiding cover for birds and other wildlife, but its thin branches are not ideal for most nesting birds. The 1/4-inch, red, egg-shaped fruits split open when ripe to reveal two to four scarlet arils. These are eaten by birds. Flowering is most extensive in winter and spring, while fruits are most abundant during summer and fall.

Florida boxwood (*Schaefferia frutescens*) is a 30-foot-tall, semi-deciduous tree that occurs naturally in Florida only in coastal hammocks of extreme south Florida. Like others in this family, the thin stems do not provide ideal nesting sites for many birds, but the foliage creates some hiding cover. Like false boxwood (*Gyminda latifolia*) above, Florida boxwood is also dioecious. Flowering mostly occurs in spring, with the red, 1/4-inch fruits ripening mostly in late summer.

Chrysobalanaceae (Coco-plum family)

This family contains only two species in eastern North America, both occurring in Florida. Both have rounded, evergreen leaves and succulent, edible fruit. One of these, gopher apple (*Licania michauxii*), is a woody ground cover. The other species is described here.

Coco-plum (*Chrysobalanus icaco*) occurs as two distinct forms. Sometimes it is an upright shrub (to about 15 feet in height) with dark green foliage and a rounded crown. The other form is a horizontal, woody ground cover. It occurs throughout south Florida in moist soil communities of coastal and inland habitats, although it will adapt to drier soils. Coco-plum is an excellent wildlife plant for regions of the state that do not regularly freeze. Upright forms are good wildlife cover and both forms are superb food producers. The small, greenish flowers attract many pollinating insects, while the "plums" are round, about 1/2 inch in diameter, dark purple (sometimes whitish), and sweet tasting. Many species of wildlife relish them. Fruits are produced nearly year-round. In addition to its ornamental and wildlife value, the fruits were an important food source for the Seminole Indians and are still used in jellies and preserves.

Cornaceae (Dogwood family)

Dogwoods are deciduous shrubs or small trees often prized in the landscape for their ornamental flowers and fall color. They also produce succulent fruits that are eaten by a wide variety of wildlife. All species in Florida belong to the dogwood genus, *Cornus*.

Pagoda dogwood/alternate-leaved dogwood (*C. alternifolia*) is so named because all other native dogwoods have opposite leaves. This multi-stemmed shrub or small tree may reach 30 feet in height in northeastern states, but it is smaller here. Pagoda dogwood is

rare in Florida and restricted to a few river bluff woodlands in the Panhandle. As an understory planting in a naturalized landscape and within its natural range, this shrub has many desirable characteristics. The broad clusters of creamy white flowers in the spring give way to deep blue, 1/4-inch fruits on reddish stalks in early fall.

Silky dogwood (*C. amomum*) is another shrubby dogwood with a very limited natural distribution in the Florida Panhandle. This species occurs in wet and moist soil habitats near streams and wetlands, and does best when used in landscapes where it receives adequate soil moisture and fertility. Stems of this plant are covered with fine silky hairs; hence, its name. Flowers are white and in clusters, while the 1/4- to 1/3-inch fruits are pale blue or whitish.

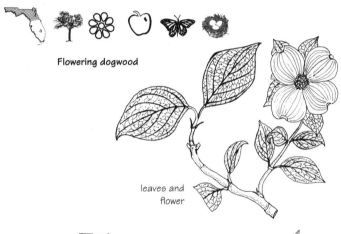

Flowering dogwood

leaves and
flower

Flowering dogwood (*C. florida*) is one of the most widely planted ornamental native trees and a symbol of southern landscapes. Many gardeners are unaware that it is also a useful wildlife plant. The branches of this small (to about 40 feet), graceful tree help support the nests of many songbirds. The small flowers, which are surrounded by large showy bracts, produce 1/2-inch-long, red, egg-shaped fruits by fall that are eagerly consumed by many birds and mammals. In Florida, flowering dogwood occurs mostly in well-drained, slightly acidic, sandy soils in north and central counties. It should not be attempted south of its natural range, and care should be taken to use only specimens raised from Florida stock, as others may not perform well in this climate.

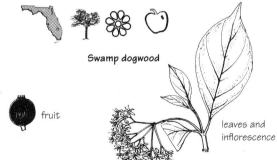

Swamp dogwood

fruit

leaves and
inflorescence

Swamp dogwood (*C. foemina*) is a multi-trunked tree that rarely exceeds 15 feet in height. As its name implies, it generally occurs in wetland habitats, but it will adapt to drier conditions in the home landscape once established. This dogwood has the widest natural range in Florida, occurring in pockets even into south Florida. Swamp dogwood has many clusters of white flowers in the spring and large clusters of 1/4-inch, pale blue fruits in the fall. Although an excellent food plant, its weak branches and relatively open character create only moderate cover.

Cupressaceae (Cypress family)

This large family of evergreens does not include the bald cypress as the name might suggest, but the true cypresses native to many western states. In Florida, this family is represented by two genera—the white and red cedars. These species are medium-sized trees with scalelike leaves. The dense and somewhat spiny foliage provides excellent cover for wildlife.

Atlantic white cedar (*Chamaecyparis thyoides*) is a long-lived, 60- to 90-foot tree that—within the state—is restricted to acidic freshwater swamps in north and north-central Florida. It once occurred in dense stands, but its range and numbers have been greatly reduced by past timber practices. Atlantic white cedar produces small, bluish purple cones, each containing 1/10-inch to 1/5-inch-long winged seeds. These ripen by fall, but have very limited value as wildlife food.

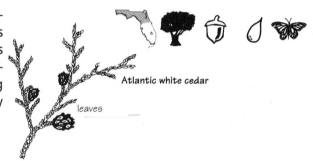

Atlantic white cedar

leaves

Southern red cedar (*Juniperus silicicola*) is a greatly adaptable species that occurs naturally throughout north and central Florida in nearly every type of growing condition including coastal habitats. This long-lived, but slow-growing, dioecious tree may eventually reach 60 feet in height, and it retains its somewhat pyramidal shape throughout. As it matures, the distinctive reddish, scaly bark enhances its ornamental character. Southern red cedar is one of the best native trees for providing wildlife cover because of its dense, somewhat spiny foliage. The 1/3-inch, bluish gray fruits, which ripen in the fall on female trees, are eaten by a variety of birds, but fruit production varies each year. Southern red cedar should not be planted

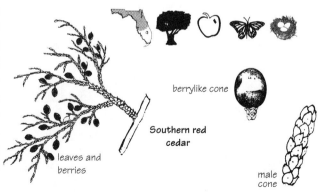

berrylike cone

Southern red cedar

leaves and berries

male cone

in landscapes near hawthorns or crabapples because it serves as a host for cedar-apple rust disease.

Ebenaceae (Ebony family)

This is a mostly tropical family that includes the ebony tree. In Florida, it is represented by only one species.

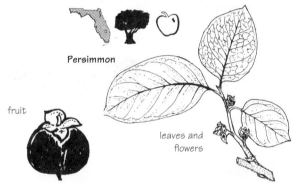

Persimmon

fruit

leaves and flowers

Persimmon (*Diospyros virginiana*) is a 40- to 60-foot deciduous tree that occurs naturally throughout Florida except the Keys. Although it is adaptable to a variety of upland sites, it is especially good at colonizing disturbed places and often is found growing in dense stands along roadways and cleared areas. This tree will produce underground suckers and spread, if allowed to. Persimmons are dioecious, so only the females produce the 2-inch, orangish fruits, which are sometimes grown commercially. The fruits are especially attractive to medium-sized mammals such as raccoons and opossums. The trees have average cover value to wildlife.

Ericaceae (Blueberry family)

Although this large family contains some of the most commonly used landscape ornamentals, such as azaleas, rhododendrons, and mountain laurel, only the native blueberries and huckleberries will be described here as wildlife plants. These species have numerous attractive, white, bell-shaped flowers in spring, and round, blue or purple, succulent fruit in summer or fall. Some are important commercially as human food. All members require acid soils. They have extremely fine root systems. Container-grown specimens require many months to become established following planting.

HUCKLEBERRIES (*Gaylussacia* spp.) are small deciduous shrubs that differ very little from true blueberries. Three species are native to Florida and all spread by underground runners. Fruits for all species ripen in late summer or early fall and are about 1/4 inch in diameter.

Dwarf huckleberry (*Gaylussacia dumosa*) is a woody ground cover that rarely exceeds 1 foot in height. It normally occurs in well-drained pinelands, where it forms clumps. This huckleberry is native to north and central Florida. The small, sweet black fruits ripen in the fall and are favored by many wildlife.

Dangleberry (*G. tomentosa*, syn. *G. frondosa*) is a shrub to 6 feet in height that occurs in wet and well-drained pineland soils in north and central Florida. Its wide-spreading branches offer little cover, but its sweet, dark blue fruits are readily eaten by wildlife.

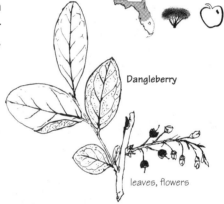

Dangleberry

fruit

leaves, flowers

Mosier's huckleberry (*G. mosieri*) is a low-growing shrub that may reach 1 1/2 feet in height. It occurs within the Panhandle in wet and seasonally wet soils. Most noticeable about this huckleberry are the many silky hairs that cover the new stem growth, flower tubes, and even the black fruits. The fruits are bland, but are eaten by wildlife.

BLUEBERRIES (*Vaccinium* spp.) are a complex collection of woody plants that vary greatly within species. Natural hybrids can occur, and differentiating species can be diffi-cult at times. Blueberries spread by underground runners, but the extent of this differs among species. All produce the typical fruit, but not all produce sweet fruit, and fruit size differs among species. A total of six distinct species are included here.

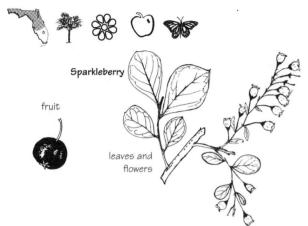

Sparkleberry

fruit

leaves and flowers

Sparkleberry (*Vaccinium arboreum*) is a shrubby, deciduous tree that may reach 30 feet in height. Native to north and central Florida, it occurs in a variety of habitats from moist hammocks to sand pine scrubs. It tolerates a broader range of soil pH than other blueberries, but still prefers acidic conditions. Sparkleberry has many aesthetic qualities. Its slender twisting trunk and branches give it form and texture, as does its rust-colored, peeling bark. In late spring, the trees are covered in fragrant, bell-shaped blooms that attract a wide variety of butterflies, bees, and other pollinators. By fall, the 1/4-inch, black fruits are ripe, and the leaves have turned reddish. Although the fruits are a bit bland, they are readily eaten by wildlife. Sparkleberry seems to do best when planted in filtered sunlight or where it receives sun for only part of the day.

Highbush blueberry (*V. corymbosum*) is the parent of all commercial blueberries grown in eastern North America. Throughout this range, it is extremely variable, and taxonomists have placed some Florida forms as separate species, most noticeably *V. elliottii*. For the purposes of this book, I have followed more recent convention and lumped all highbush blueberries under *V. corymbosum*. Highbush blueberry occurs naturally in north and central Florida in a variety of wet to well-drained habitats with acidic soils. It is a multi-stemmed, deciduous shrub that can reach 12 feet in height. It will also sometimes sucker and form small clumps, especially if the ground is disturbed around it. The sweet, 1/4- to 1/3-inch berries ripen in early summer and vary in color from powdery blue to black. Few fruits attract the attention of wildlife more than those of this shrub. It also provides some cover value once the plant becomes mature. Highbush blueberry will grow in a shady understory location, but fruit production is greatly enhanced if it receives at least a half-day of sun.

derstory location, but fruit production is greatly enhanced if it receives at least a half-day of sun.

Little blueberry (*V. darrowi*) is one of two species of small, evergreen blueberries that rarely exceed 3 feet in height. It occurs from north to south-central Florida in well-drained, sandy soil and in seasonally wet pinelands with acidic soils. It often spreads by underground suckers and forms localized colonies. Little blueberry has small, blue-green leaves. The 1/4-inch, sweet fruits are powdery blue and ripen during the early summer. This, and shiny blueberry described next, makes an excellent ground cover for sunny or partly sunny locations, given the proper pH conditions.

Shiny blueberry (*V. myrsinites*) is very similar to little blueberry in growth characteristics and distribution. They often occur together on the same site. Shiny blueberry, however, has small, bright green leaves, and the sweet fruits are shiny black.

Deerberry (*V. stamineum*) is a deciduous shrub that may reach 15 feet in height. It has an open growth habit that enhances its ornamental value, but reduces its ability to provide wildlife cover. Deerberry occurs mostly in the understory of open woodlands with well-drained sandy soils. It ranges from north to south-central Florida. In the spring, it produces a mass of open, bell-shaped, white flowers that hang from the branches on pronounced stalks. The mature, 1/3- to 1/2-inch fruits vary in color from pink, amber, and reddish to blue and dark purple. They are not sweet, but are readily eaten by wildlife after they ripen in summer.

Lowbush blueberry (*V. tenellum*) is a 1-foot-tall, deciduous shrub that spreads by underground runners, often forming localized clones. In Florida, its range is limited to Clay County (northeast Florida) in well-drained, sandy soils. The sweet, 1/4-inch, purple fruits ripen in summer. Although an excellent wildlife ground cover, its limited natural range in Florida restricts its usefulness.

Euphorbiaceae (Spurge family)

This very large family contains many non-native species that are important either commercially or ornamentally, such as the rubber, tung, and castor-bean trees, and the shrubby crotons. It also includes many common lawn "weeds" such as the spurges and the tread-softly or stinging nettle (*Cnidosculus* spp.). Some euphorbias, such as the castor bean and the infamous south Florida native manchineel tree (*Hippomane mancinella*), produce complex poisonous chemicals. Only one genus of woody plants in Florida, the milkbarks (*Drypetes*), has much significance to wildlife. Milkbarks are small, tropical, dioecious, evergreen trees confined to south Florida. Female trees produce a rounded fruit. The sap of these trees is "milky"—hence, the common name.

Milkbark (*Drypetes diversifolia*) is a 30-foot-tall tree that is common in the hammocks of the Keys, but is less common on the peninsula of extreme south Florida. The milk-white bark and the shiny, dark-green, 3- to 5-inch, oval leaves give this tree some aesthetic character. The white fruits are 1/2 to 1 inch in diameter and may not ripen until spring—nearly a year after flowering. The fruits are used by a variety of mammals and some birds, and the dense foliage provides cover. This species commonly produces root suckers that will spread over a wide area if allowed to.

Guiana plum (*D. laterifolia*) is a 30-foot-tall tree whose natural range includes eastern coastal hammocks from Brevard County through the Keys. This species differs in several respects from milkbark. The bark is light brown with a reddish tinge. Flowering occurs between January and April, and the reddish, 1/4-inch-diameter, rounded, hairy fruits ripen by fall. This tree's tolerance to partial shade, salt, alkaline soils, and moderate cold make it adaptable to south Florida landscapes. Its wildlife value, however, is only marginal.

Fagaceae (Oak family)

This family is well-represented in Florida and contains many well-known species that are commonly used in urban landscapes. Besides the 23 species of native oaks, the family also includes beeches and chestnuts. Members of this family produce calorie-rich nuts that are important to the diet of many species of wildlife, but especially to mammals such as squirrels and other rodents, raccoons, opossums, and white-tailed deer. Birds such as jays, bobwhite quail, and wild turkey also use the nuts of some of these species. Oaks in particular take a dominant role in the flora of many of Florida's natural communities. Urban landscapes, however, often fail to take advantage of the great diversity of this family and have relied too frequently on a handful of species.

Chinkapin (*Castanea pumila*, syn. *C. alnifolia*) is a shrubby, deciduous tree that rarely exceeds 20 feet in height. A close relative of the American chestnut (*C. dentata*), chinkapins have elliptical, deeply toothed leaves and linear stalks of small fragrant flowers. Flowering occurs during the spring and summer, and the 3/4-inch-long nuts mature in the fall. The one or two sweet nuts enclosed in spiny, burlike husks are eagerly sought by many wildlife species. Chinkapin occurs mostly on well-drained soils in relatively open habitats from north to north-central Florida. Because they often form dense clumps from underground runners, this plant also is excellent at providing wildlife cover. This attractive and valuable native should be made much more available from the nursery trade than it currently is.

American beech (*Fagus grandifolia*) is a major component of the eastern deciduous forest in North America, but its natural range in Florida is confined mostly to the Panhandle and a few scattered hammocks in the northeast. It is not adaptable to Florida landscapes much beyond its natural range. This is a large, long-lived, deciduous tree that may reach 100 feet at maturity, but its growth rate is relatively slow. It also may reproduce by root suckers and produce small groves, if allowed to do so. Because it is adapted to reproducing in the dense shade of the oak-hickory forest, young beeches do best when planted in a location that receives partial shade. It will eventually grow to become the dominant shade tree. American beech

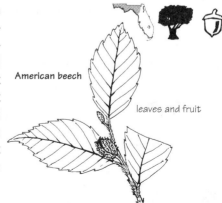

American beech

leaves and fruit

grows best in moist, fertile soils. Its large crown and branches provide cover for many woodland wildlife species, and the 3/4-inch, triangular beech nuts that ripen in the fall are a relished food source.

OAKS (*Quercus* spp.) are a varied group of woody plants that includes both trees and shrubs. Identification of individual oaks sometimes is difficult because leaf shapes may differ greatly even on the same tree. Hybridization between species also may occur.

In general, oaks provide good wildlife cover. They also provide an important food source with their acorns, but this varies greatly among species. Many oaks do not produce dependable crops each year, but follow a good year with several years of almost no production. Acorn size is variable among species. Although mammals are able to eat acorns of any size, birds often must swallow them whole, and small birds such as quail are unable to eat those that are too large. Acorns also vary in their bitterness. Not all oaks produce acorns that taste "sweet". As a rule, oaks in the "white" oak group produce "sweeter" acorns than those in the "red" oak group, because their acorns often are lower in tannic acid. Generally, wildlife prefer to eat the "sweeter" acorns. As a very general rule, white oaks have leaves with rounded lobes, while red oaks have leaves with pointed ones. But because some oaks have leaves without lobes, this trait is not always obvious. White oak acorns mature in the fall of their first year, while red oak acorns do not mature until their second fall.

To help the reader a bit, I have organized the oak species into the two different groups and have arranged each group alphabetically by scientific name.

WHITE OAKS

White oak

acorn

leaves

White oak (*Quercus alba*) occurs in Florida only in the northern Panhandle region in moist fertile soils. This straight-trunked, deciduous tree has a broad, round crown and may reach 100 feet in height. The distinctive, lobed leaves turn wine red in fall and brown in winter. The brown leaves often are held on the tree until spring. The acorns are 1/2 to 3/4 of an inch long, and large crops are produced every four to six years.

Bluff oak (*Q. austrina*) may reach 100 feet at maturity and has an irregular and narrow crown. It occurs throughout northern Florida, most often in well-drained, alkaline, woodland soils. Leaves are lobed somewhat like those of white oak (*Q. alba*), but they vary greatly throughout the tree. The lobes also tend to "droop". The acorns are 1/2 to 3/4 of an inch long. Large crops are produced every four to six years.

Chapman oak (*Q. chapmanii*) is a small (to about 30 feet), deciduous oak common to well-drained, sandy soil areas throughout Florida, except the Keys. The slightly lobed to oval leaves are absent for only a brief period during the winter. It has a broad-spreading crown and irregular branches. The acorns are quite broad and 3/4 to 1 inch in length. Good crops are produced every two to three years.

Sand live oak (*Q. geminata*) is considered a subspecies of the live oak (*Q. virginiana*) by some taxonomists, but I've chosen to agree with others who give it separate species status, because its characteristics are certainly distinct. This tree is found throughout Florida, except the Keys, in deep, well-drained, sandy soils, including coastal dunes. Its mature height rarely exceeds 40 feet and is often less than 30. When grown as a specimen, it has the same picturesque growth form as live oak (*Q. virginiana*), but in miniature. If allowed to, however, it will sucker and form thickets. Small, evergreen, linear leaves, often curled under at the margins and hairy beneath, are held on small, stiff branches. Acorns are linear, about 1 inch long, and large crops generally are dependable each year.

Overcup oak (*Q. lyrata*) is a 90-foot-tall, deciduous tree, native to bottomland forest habitats west of the Suwannee River in the Panhandle. This tree has a tall, straight trunk and a broad, rounded crown. Leaves are similar in shape to those of white oak (*Q. alba*), but they are longer and more linear. The acorns are round and slightly flattened, and between 3/4 of an inch and 1 inch in size. They are nearly totally enclosed by the cup—hence, its common name. Good acorn crops occur only every three or four years. Overcup oaks are slow-growing, but long-lived, trees. They grow well in poorly drained soils.

Sand post oak (*Q. margaretta*) often is considered to be a subspecies of post oak (*Q. stellata*), but again I side with those that give it separate species status. This is a medium-tall (rarely more than 50 feet), deciduous tree that occurs mostly on well-drained, sandy soils within sandhill communities in north and central Florida. Sand post oaks have an irregular shape and crown. The leaves are more irregular and rarely exhibit the distinctive crucifix shape seen in the post oak (*Q. stellata*). Acorns are rather large, usually about 1 inch in length, and good production occurs every three to four years.

Swamp chestnut oak

leaves

acorns

Swamp chestnut oak (*Q. michauxii*) is a large (to 100 feet), deciduous tree that occurs mostly in moist, fertile soils in north and north-central Florida. Its crown is relatively narrow, but its height and enormous, oval, many-lobed leaves enable it to dominate the area where it is growing. The leaves turn wine-red in the fall. Acorns generally are 1 to 1 1/2 inches in length, and large crops occur sporadically, usually every four to five years. This tree does well on alkaline soil and will tolerate flooding for brief periods.

Dwarf live oak (*Q. minima*) is an evergreen, 3-foot-tall shrub that forms extensive clones by underground runners. Because of this, it acts more like a ground cover than a shrub. The leaves are stiff, leathery, and extremely variable in shape. Most are long and linear, but others have poorly defined lobes and may be spiny. This oak occurs mostly in open, sandy pinelands from north to south-central Florida. Acorns are narrow and rather large, between 3/4 of an inch and 1 inch in length. Good crops generally occur every two to three years. Given the proper location, this oak can make an excellent cover thicket for wildlife.

Chinkapin oak/chinquapin oak (*Q. muehlenbergii*) is a 60-foot-tall, deciduous tree, native to a small region of the western Panhandle, usually found on well-drained, alkaline, woodland soil. This oak has leaves similar to swamp chestnut oak (*Q. michauxii*), but they are more linear, and they are pointed at the tip. The crown is rounded, and its growth is rather rapid, especially when young. Acorns are 1/2 to 1 inch in length, conical in shape, and good crops are produced every three to four years. Fall color is a rather bland, mottled yellow.

Running oak (*Q. pumila*) is similar to dwarf live oak (*Q. minima*), as it is also a low-growing shrub that often forms extensive thickets by underground runners. In fact, both species often grow in close proximity to each other in open, sandy pineland habitats in north and central Florida. This oak, however, is deciduous, and its leaves are almost always thin and linear. Also different are the acorns. Running oak has small, rounded acorns, normally about 1/4 inch long, that are useful to a wide variety of small birds in addition to other wildlife.

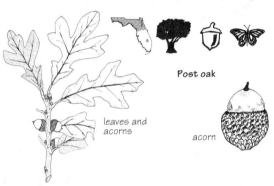

Post oak

leaves and
acorns

acorn

Post oak (*Q. stellata*) is a medium-sized (about 60 feet), deciduous tree native to sandy, alkaline soils in north and north-central Florida. One of the most distinctive features of this tree is its glossy green leaves that usually are shaped like a crucifix. Post oaks are stout, short-limbed trees with rounded crowns. They also are slow-growing, but long-lived. Acorns are 1/2 to 1 inch in length, and good crops are produced every two to four years. I believe that this is one of the most distinctive and visually interesting of Florida's native oaks, and its lack of use in developed landscapes is regrettable.

Live oak (*Q. virginiana*) is the symbol of the southern landscape and requires little description here. Because of its broad crown, impressive size, and evergreen nature, this tree provides cover for many species of wildlife, and its large sprawling branches are used mostly by owls and blue jays. The outer branches, often draped in Spanish moss, provide nesting cover for orchard orioles, painted buntings, and northern parula warblers. It is adaptable to a wide range of soil and water conditions, including salt tolerance, and its natural range extends even through the Florida Keys. Live oak is important as a food source because its 1-inch acorns are produced in abundance nearly every year. Although sometimes criticized as being a slow-grower, live oaks grow rather quickly when young and are especially long-lived.

RED OAKS

Arkansas oak (*Q. arkansana*) is a 50-foot-tall, deciduous tree found in scattered localities in the western Panhandle in well-drained, rocky or sandy soils. It has a narrow, irregular crown and dark, deeply furrowed bark. Its distinctive 2- to 3-inch leaves are broadly spatula-shaped and generally without lobes. Acorns are 1/4 to 1/3 of an inch long and rather rounded. Their small size makes them easily used by smaller birds, and acorn crops are generally dependable annually.

Southern red oak (*Q. falcata*) is a large (to about 90 feet), deciduous tree that generally is considered to consist of two distinct subspecies—*Q.f.* var. *falcata*, the Spanish or southern red oak, and *Q.f.* var. *pagodifolia*, the cherrybark oak. Because both species are very similar in their growth form and wildlife value, I will combine the two in this discussion. The southern red oak subspecies occurs throughout northern Florida in well-drained, upland sites, while the cherrybark subspecies grows only in the Panhandle west of the Apalachicola River in moist, floodplain forests. The leaves have sharply pointed lobes and turn a rich red in the autumn. The long, straight trunk supports a broad, rounded crown. The rounded acorns are about a 1/2 inch in length and are produced in dependable annual crops.

Bluejack oak (*Q. incana*) is a medium-sized (to about 40 feet), deciduous tree with an irregular trunk and open crown. The linear, willow-shaped leaves are bluish green. In spring, the new growth is pinkish. Bluejack oaks most frequently occur in dry, sandy, open woods throughout north and central Florida, often with longleaf pine and turkey oak. The rounded acorns are about a 1/2 inch in length, and production is fairly reliable each year. This oak is rather fast growing, but short lived.

Inopina oak (*Q. inopina*) is the only oak endemic to Florida. It is a small (usually no more than 10 feet), evergreen, shrubby tree confined to deep, well-drained, sandy soils in central peninsular Florida. The stiff, rounded leaves are held upwards from the branches and curl tightly inward—adaptations to conserve water. Like many of the other oaks of Florida's scrub community, it will sucker and form thickets. Such thickets provide excellent escape cover, but the short branches are not good for most nesting birds. Acorns are rounded and about 1/2 inch in length.

Turkey oak (*Q. laevis*) is a 40- to 50-foot-tall, deciduous tree, common to well-drained, sandy soils throughout north and central Florida. Like bluejack oak (*Q. incana*), it is fast-growing, but short-lived, and has an open, irregular shape. The yellow-green leaves normally have three or five sharply pointed lobes, shaped like the outline of a turkey's foot. The leaves turn dark red in late fall. The rounded acorns are about 1 inch long and are produced abundantly only every two to three years.

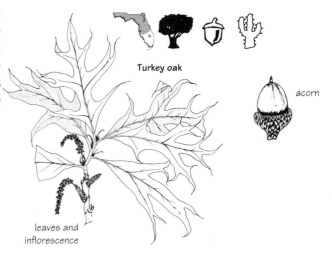

Turkey oak

acorn

leaves and inflorescence

Laurel oak (*Q. laurifolia*) is perhaps the most widely planted oak around urban developments in Florida. The diamond-leaf oak (*Q. hemispherica*), whose separate species status is under debate by taxonomists, has growth form and wildlife value identical to laurel oak. Native to moist forest soils throughout the state north of the Everglades, laurel oak is adaptable and fast growing. Laurel oaks are so quick to mature that they may produce acorns within 15 years of age, but they rarely survive more than 100 years. This deciduous tree may reach 100 feet in height. Trunks are straight, and the crowns are broad and round. Leaves are linear and without much fall color. Acorns are rounded, about 1 inch in length, and good crops are produced annually.

Blackjack oak (*Q. marilandica*) is a 30- to 40-foot-tall, deciduous tree, native to poorly drained, rather barren soils in the Panhandle. This slow-growing, short-lived, shrubby tree tolerates alkaline and droughty soils with a hard pan below the surface. Although rarely

used in developed landscapes, blackjack oak has distinctive, broad, spatula-shaped leaves that are sometimes three-lobed. The rounded acorns are 3/4 of an inch to 1 inch in length and good crops generally are produced annually.

Myrtle oak (*Q. myrtifolia*) is a round, evergreen, shrubby tree that rarely exceeds 30 feet in height. Native to deep sandy soils from north to south Florida, including coastal dunes, it frequently will form thickets from root suckering. Such areas provide dense cover for wildlife. Myrtle oak has small, rounded, glossy leaves that are leathery and stiff. The small (1/4 to 1/2 inch), round acorns are produced reliably each year.

Water oak (*Q. nigra*) is a common, 60-foot-tall, deciduous tree that occurs in north and central Florida in a variety of moist soil habitats. A rapid-growing, but generally short-lived tree, it has a tall, straight trunk and a rounded crown. The leaves are rather small and often spatula shaped (sometimes lobed). The rounded acorns are variable in size, but normally are 1/2 to 3/4 of an inch in length. Good production occurs every one to two years.

Willow oak (*Q. phellos*) is a 70- to 80-foot-tall, deciduous tree, native to the western Panhandle and a small region of the northeastern peninsula. Although its best growth occurs in fertile bottomland soils, it is fairly adaptable. Willow oak will tolerate flooded soils for several weeks at a time without problems. Named for its linear, willowlike leaves, this oak has rather rapid growth and is long-lived. It also produces large, reliable crops of 1/2-inch-long, rounded acorns annually.

Shumard oak (*Q. shumardii*) is a large (about 70 feet), deciduous tree, native to north Florida in moist woodland habitats. It is tolerant of alkaline soils. One of the most attractive oaks within its range, the shumard oak has a tall, straight trunk and a broad, rounded crown. The shiny dark green leaves have seven, nine, or eleven deeply cut and sharply pointed lobes, and turn a rich red in late fall after the first frost. The acorns are rounded and between 1/2 inch and 1 inch in length. Good crops are produced every two to four years.

Black oak (*Q. velutina*) is a 60-foot-tall, deciduous tree that is common throughout eastern North America, but has a very limited distribution in the north-central Florida Panhandle. In this area of Florida, it prefers fertile, upland soils, often with a clay subsoil. The trees have an open, somewhat irregular, crown, and branches occur low on the trunk. Black oak has leaves that are less deeply lobed than shumard oak (*Q. shumardii*), and fall color is less intense. The rounded acorns are between 1/2 and 3/4 of an inch in length, and good crops are produced every two to three years. This is not a tree with wide landscape applications in Florida. Other red oaks with similar wildlife characteristics normally would be better choices.

Goodeniaceae (Inkberry family)

This family is mostly Australian in distribution and contains only one genus with one species native to Florida. A second species (*Scaevola frutescens*), with the same common name as the native species, is widely planted in Florida as an ornamental.

Inkberry (*Scaevola plumieri*) is a dense succulent shrub that rarely exceeds 4 feet in height. Native to the coastal dunes of south and south-central Florida, it is an important, but often neglected, component of the dune-stabilizing ecosystem. Its stems often trail across the sand and will root if left undisturbed. The leaves are thick and fleshy, 1 to 1 1/2 inches long, and grow mostly at the branch tips where they form rosettes. Flowers are borne in small clusters among the terminal leaves during most months. They are white and composed of five or six lobes, spread out fan-shaped. Within several months, the flowers give way to 1/2-inch, dark black fruits. These are eaten mostly by small mammals within native beach systems, but hold some interest for birds when used in other settings. Although inkberry is ideally used in coastal landscapes at elevations near high tide, it is adaptable to other areas.

Hamamelidaceae (Witch-hazel family)

This family is represented by three genera of deciduous trees and shrubs in Florida. One, the witch alders, represented by *Fothergilla gardeni*, is not described because it has little value to wildlife. The others, each represented by only one species, are somewhat better wildlife plants.

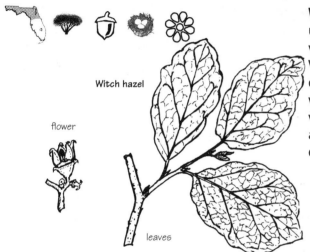

Witch hazel

flower

leaves

Witch hazel (*Hamamelis virginiana*) is a multi-stemmed shrub native to upland wooded areas of north and central Florida. Although tolerant of a variety of conditions, it does best under partial shade in fertile, acidic soil. Witch hazel is slow growing, but may eventually reach 25 feet in height. Its dense branches of very heavy wood provide excellent cover for small wildlife prior to leaf-fall, but the 1/3-inch-long, hard seeds have minor food value. Distinctive are the leaves, which turn a brilliant yellow early in fall, and the spidery, aromatic blooms that appear once the lower leaves have dropped.

Sweet gum (*Liquidambar styraciflua*) is a commonly planted shade tree that may reach more than 120 feet in height. Native to north and central regions of Florida, it is abundant in wet and poorly drained soils, but is adaptable. These tall, strongly branched trees provide good cover in their narrow canopy, but the flattened, 1/3-inch-long, hard seeds, produced in numerous very spiny seed balls, have minimal food value. Sweet gum is susceptible to a variety of insect pests in the southern portion of its range that reduce the attractiveness of its foliage and its growth rate. In central Florida especially, care should be taken to use specimens grown from local sources.

Juglandaceae (Hickory family)

The hickories and walnuts are a group of large, deciduous trees characterized by feather-like, compound leaves, dense, heavy wood, and the production of hard-shelled nuts. These trees are often a dominant component of the plant community in which they occur. The crowns and strong branches provide excellent cover for wildlife living in woodland canopies. The oil-rich nuts are a prized food source mostly for mammals, and particularly for squirrels and other woodland rodents. Nut crops are annually abundant once the trees mature. One walnut (*Juglans* spp.) and several hickories (*Carya* spp.) occur in Florida in a wide variety of conditions.

Water hickory (*Carya aquatica*) is a large tree native to wetland forest habitats from north to south-central Florida. The straight tall trunks support a somewhat narrow, irregular crown and, unlike other members of this family, the wood is rather weak. Leaves are composed of seven to seventeen very narrow leaflets. The nuts, 1 to 1 1/2 inches long, have a rather thin shell, but the kernels are very bitter and are not very attractive to wildlife. Water hickory is a useful canopy tree for moist soil areas that do not flood for extended periods, but other hickories are more useful to wildlife and should be used where appropriate.

Bitternut hickory (*C. cordiformis*) is another tall hickory with thin-shelled, bitter-tasting, 1- to 1 1/2-inch-long nuts that occurs in floodplain forests. Its range in Florida, however, is confined to only a few major river drainages in the Panhandle. Because of this, its use in Florida landscapes is greatly restricted. Bitternut hickory produces good nut crops only every three to four years.

Scrub hickory (*C. floridana*) is a medium-sized (to 60 feet), often multi-trunked tree native to deep, well-drained sands of central Florida. It has a short, straight trunk, but its crooked, twisting branches and wide-spreading crown give it character. Leaves usually are composed of three or five leaflets, sometimes seven, and are yellowish green in color. The thick-

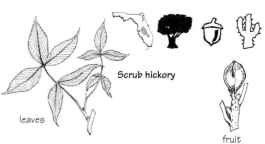

leaves

Scrub hickory

fruit

shelled nuts, 1 to 1 1/2 inches long, have sweet kernels and are eagerly sought by wildlife. This is an excellent hickory for sandy areas, including coastal dunes.

Pignut hickory (*C. glabra*) is, in many respects, a much larger version of scrub hickory (*C. floridana*), and is native to woodland habitats of north and central Florida. This tree may reach more than 100 feet in height in fertile, upland soil. Pignut hickory has a large, straight trunk and broad, rounded crown that provides good cover. Leaves usually have five or seven leaflets that are deep green. The 1- to 2-inch-long nuts have a relatively thick shell, but less so than scrub hickory. The sweetness of the kernels varies greatly. Pignut hickory has the best fall color among Florida species, turning a bright yellow in late fall.

Sand hickory (*C. pallida*) is a 30- to 50-foot tree native to sandy upland soils in the western and central Panhandle. It is similar in appearance to pignut hickory (*C. glabra*), but the undersides of the leaves are much paler, and the smaller nuts (1/2 inch to 1 1/2 inches long) have a thin shell. The kernels are sweet and eagerly sought by wildlife. This hickory has good wildlife value, but its limited range in Florida reduces its potential use. Regrettably, it also is not easily available at present from the nursery trade.

Mockernut hickory (*C. tomentosa*) is another large (to 100 feet) hickory with a tall, straight trunk and rounded crown. The undersides of the leaflets (normally seven per leaf) and the leaf stems are tomentose (i.e., fuzzy)—hence, the scientific name. The common name is derived from the difficulty that early settlers had in cracking the thick shells of the nuts. The kernels are sweet, but difficult for most animals except rodents to eat. They are also large: between 1 1/2 and 3 inches long. Mockernut hickory is native to fertile upland soils of north Florida and is not recommended for areas beyond this range.

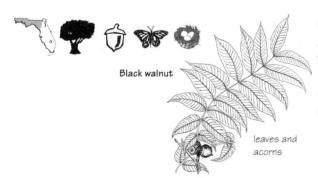

Black walnut

leaves and acorns

Black walnut (*Juglans nigra*) is the most widespread walnut in North America, but its range in Florida is restricted to fertile woodland areas of the central Panhandle. This beautiful, tall tree often exceeds 100 feet in height, and the dense, rounded crown and sturdy branches provide good cover. Black walnut is renowned for the quality of its wood, and the nuts are rich in oils and have a distinctive flavor. The 1 1/4- to 2-inch-long nuts are mostly used by squirrels and other woodland rodents because the tough shells are difficult for other animals to crack.

Lauraceae (Bay family)

The laurel family is a large family of plants distributed worldwide. Many of them are economically important because of their fragrant wood and leaves, or their berrylike fruit, which consists normally of a fleshy outer part, rich in oils, covering a hard inner seed. Non-native members of this family include the cinnamon, true bay, camphor, and avocado trees. Six genera of trees and shrubs native to Florida have important wildlife value and are discussed here. Most members of this family also serve as larval food for spicebush and palamedes swallowtail butterflies, making them important components of a butterfly garden.

Gulf licaria (*Licaria triandra*) is a small, tropical, evergreen tree, extremely rare in Florida and naturally confined to areas near Miami. Its large leaves, oval-shaped with pronounced tips, create good wildlife cover. The inconspicuous flowers bloom in June, and 1/2-inch, purplish black fruits ripen by the following spring. They are shaped somewhat like acorns, enclosed in a red, cuplike base. The fruit is eaten by many birds and mammals. This tree could be used in a variety of upland habitats in frost-free areas of south Florida.

Spicebush (*Lindera benzoin*) is a 6- to 10-foot-tall, deciduous shrub native to moist woodland understories in north Florida. As its name suggests, its leaves and stems emit a spicy aroma when crushed. Its open branching pattern is attractive, but does not create good wildlife cover. Dense clusters of pale yellow flowers appear before the leaves in early spring. Spicebush is dioecious, so only female plants produce the bright red, 1/3-inch-long fruits, which ripen by September. The fruits are especially attractive to many songbirds. In fall, leaves turn a brilliant yellow. Spicebush is an interesting and useful accent for naturalized landscapes within its natural range and in soils that are fertile, moist, and slightly alkaline.

Jove's fruit (*Lindera melissaefolium*) is an extremely rare 1- to 2-foot-tall spicebush native to swampy acidic depressions in local areas of the Florida Panhandle. Because of its limited range and specific soil requirements, it is not a likely candidate for use in the landscape. Its wildlife value and characteristics are similar, however, to that of spicebush (*L. benzoin*).

Bog spicebush (*Lindera subcoriacea*) is another extremely rare spicebush in Florida with limited landscape applications. Native to a few wet seepage areas in north Florida, it has similar wildlife values and characteristics to those of spicebush (*L. benzoin*).

Pond spice (*Litsea aestivalis*) is an uncommon, 6- to 12-foot-tall, deciduous shrub native to wet soil habitats in north Florida. Its tiny, oval leaves and thin, zig-zag stems provide little cover, but the pattern of its branching and its reddish bark are attractive. Small yellow flowers appear in spring before the leaves develop. Pond spice is dioecious. The 1/4-inch, rounded, bright red fruits ripen by fall and are used by birds. Pond spice would be a useful and attractive plant for the edge of ponds.

Lancewood (*Nectandra coriacea*) is an evergreen tree, 25 to 30 feet tall, common to moist coastal hammocks in south Florida. It is shade tolerant and has some cold tolerance. If planted along the coast, it can be used as far north as south-central areas. Lancewood often has an irregular shape with a narrowly rounded crown. The slender branches do not provide much nesting support, but the large, elliptical leaves help to give it value as hiding cover. Numerous white flowers may be produced any time between March and September, but spring and late summer peaks occur. The 1/2-inch, purplish black fruits, held in orangish red cups, ripen between late fall and winter. They are eaten by a wide variety of wildlife.

Red bay (*Persea borbonia*) is an extremely adaptable, evergreen, 40- to 60-foot-tall tree native to a variety of habitats throughout Florida. It is found growing in both upland forests and on coastal dunes. This tree has an irregular shape and broad, rounded crown. Leathery, bright green, oval leaves help create good cover. They also can be used as cooking substitutes for true bay leaves. The 1/3-inch, purple fruits ripen by early fall and are eaten by many wildlife. Red bay is a very useful and attractive tree for a wildlife land-scape. It is susceptible to a leaf gall that curls the edges of some of its leaves, but because this does not harm the tree in any way, no action should be taken to try to control it.

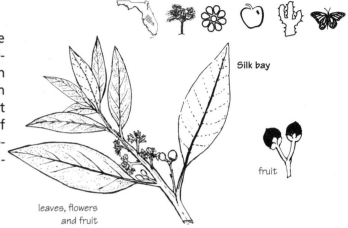

Silk bay

fruit

leaves, flowers
and fruit

Silk bay (*Persea humilis*) is considered to be a red bay subspecies by some taxonomists, but it has several features that make it distinct. This 30- to 40-foot-tall, evergreen tree occurs in deep, well-drained, sandy soil habitats in central Florida. The stems and undersides of its leaves are unique—both are covered with dense, copper-colored hairs which give the tree an almost golden appearance with the proper wind and sun conditions. The fruits of silk bay are often slightly larger than red bay (*P. borbonia*), but in other re-spects it differs very little. Silk bay should only be used in areas with well-drained soils.

Swamp bay (*Persea palustris*) also is very similar to red bay. Swamp bay is a 30- to 40-foot-tall, evergreen tree native to freshwater wetland forests throughout peninsular Florida. The leaf undersides and stems have a shaggy, reddish pubescence without the shiny character of the silk bay. This is a good tree for wet and seasonally flooded areas.

Sassafras (*Sassafras albidum*) may become a 60- to 70-foot-tall tree, but normally it is much smaller. This attractive, deciduous, dioecious species is native to sandy, well-drained habitats of north and north-central Florida. Flowers of both sexes are lemon yellow and attractive. The variable leaves often are mitten- or trident-shaped and turn red, orange, and yellow in the fall. The 1/2-inch, purplish fruits ripen by early fall on the female trees, but good fruit production only occurs every two to three years. Plant sassafras in a small grouping; it often suckers. Oils from the bark are used to make sassafras tea.

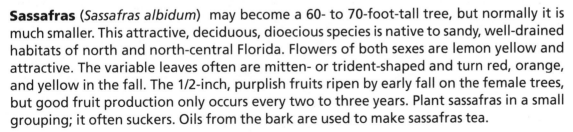

Leguminosae (Legume or Bean family)

The legumes are one of the largest families of flowering plants in the world and contain some of the world's most important food crops (beans and peas), forage crops (clover and alfalfa), and some favorite ornamentals. All produce hard, nutritious, beanlike or pealike seeds enclosed in a tough, leathery pod. Most have nitrogen-fixing bacteria associated with their root systems, which serve to enrich the soil and improve the forage quality of their foliage. Many also have showy blooms that are bee-pollinated. Four genera of native woody legumes—the acacias, locusts, tamarinds, and blackbeads—have good wildlife value. Others, such as the redbud (*Cercis canadensis*), provide little for wildlife.

ACACIAS (*Acacia* spp.) are relatively short (about 20 feet tall), broad-crowned, multi-trunked trees native to the southern half of Florida. All have crooked, thorny branches and round, yellow flower heads that are decidedly fragrant. The bean-shaped pods enclose hard seeds that are used by wildlife. Primary wildlife value, however, is from the cover that they provide. Four species occur in Florida.

Cinnecord (*Acacia choriophylla*) is a tropical tree found in Florida only on North Key Largo, but more commonly on Cuba and in the Bahamas. This is the least thorny of the native acacias, having spines only where the leaves join the stems. Leaves are shiny green and leathery, not thin and feathery like the other three native acacias. Flowering occurs most commonly in spring, but may occur in almost any month, and the flat pealike seed pods ripen several months later. Each pod contains about a dozen 1/4-inch seeds. This beautiful, but endangered, tree is adaptable to many landscape settings in frost-free areas of south Florida.

Sweet acacia (*A. farnesiana*) is the most widely distributed native acacia in Florida and can be grown from central to south Florida in sunny, well-drained coastal and interior soils. Its small, feathery leaves are deciduous for a brief period in winter, and the extremely fragrant flowers are most abundant in early spring as the new leaves develop. Flowers and the beanlike seed pods may be produced in nearly every month, however. Each pod contains about six rounded, 1/4-inch seeds. Sweet acacia is extremely thorny, with spines on the trunk, branches, and at the leaf nodes. This greatly enhances its cover value for nesting birds and other wildlife.

Long-spine acacia (*A. macracantha*) is another very rare tropical tree with a greatly restricted distribution in the Florida Keys. It also is a short tree that rarely exceeds 20 feet in height. As the name suggests, the branches and trunk are armed with long spines up to 1 1/2 inches in length. The long, feathery leaves are composed of many small leaflets. Flowering occurs mostly in the spring. Long, narrow, beanlike seed pods contain many oval, 1/4-inch seeds.

Pine acacia (*A. pinetorum*) is a shrubby tree of south Florida that normally grows in open pinelands and the edges of hammock woodlands. It is nearly identical in appearance to sweet acacia (*A. farnesiana*) and differs mostly in the size of its leaflets, which are about half the length of sweet acacia.

LOCUSTS (*Gleditsia* spp.) are large (60 to 80 feet tall), deciduous, extremely thorny trees native to bottomland forest habitats. They produce tough, flat pods that enclose many hard, oval seeds. Locusts are excellent wildlife cover plants, and their seeds are used by many mammals and some birds. Flowering occurs in the late spring, and the fruits ripen by fall. The feathery leaves have ornamental value. Both Florida species are extremely similar in most physical and biological characteristics.

Water locust (*Gleditsia aquatica*) is native from north to south-central Florida along streams and wetland habitats that undergo intermittent flooding. Seed pods are 1 to 2 inches long and contain one to three round, 1/3-inch seeds.

Water Locust

leaves

inflorescence

fruit

Honey locust (*G. triacanthos*) has a limited distribution in Florida and is found in only a few locations in the Panhandle. Although this tree occurs normally in floodplain forests, it is adaptable. The large spines are often three-forked. Thornless varieties have been developed, but these greatly reduce its wildlife cover value. Seed pods are 6 to 18 inches long and contain many round, 1/3-inch seeds.

Wild Tamarind/Lysiloma (*Lysiloma latisiliquum*, syn. *L. bahamense*) is a broad-canopied evergreen tree, between 40 and 60 feet tall, native to south Florida in a variety of upland habitats. The delicate, doubly compound leaves are composed of many 1/2-inch, light green leaflets. Numerous round, 3/4-inch clusters of fragrant, greenish white flowers bloom in the spring, while the 4- to 6-inch-long seed pods ripen by fall. The brown seed pods hang on the tree throughout winter, eventually splitting open to release the 1/2-inch seeds. The seeds are of only minor use to wildlife. Wild tamarind is tolerant of a broad range of growing conditions, including salt, and grows rapidly to become a valuable shade tree if not injured by freezing temperatures. Its canopy provides good wildlife cover, but its value as a food source is confined mostly to insect-eating species.

BLACKBEADS (*Pithecellobium* spp.) are evergreen shrubs (about 20 feet tall) native to south Florida coastal dunes, hammocks, and disturbed edges in a wide variety of soil types, making them extremely adaptable landscape choices. The leaves consist of two pairs of leaflets, and the new growth is reddish and quite attractive. Blackbeads produce many round heads of white fragrant flowers in the spring. The coiled, twisted seed pods ripen by summer. The pods split open to reveal the 1/8-inch, round, black seeds. The upper half of each seed is covered with a red fleshy aril, designed to attract birds that eat and disperse the seeds. Blackbeads have a rounded, irregular shape, and the many branches and evergreen foliage give them good cover value. Both species are larval food plants for the giant orange sulfur butterfly.

Guadeloupe blackbead (*Pithecellobium guadelupense*) occurs in extreme south Florida. It is rarely thorny.

Cat's claw (*P. unquis-cati*) has a wider distribution than guadeloupe blackbead in coastal south Florida and has more tolerance of cold temperatures. It differs also by having small, curved spines in pairs at the base of each leaf, and the leaves are smaller. Because of its thorny nature, this species provides greater cover value for wildlife.

Magnoliaceae (Magnolia family)

Magnolias (*Magnolia* spp.) in Florida are small to large trees with large leaves, relatively straight trunks, and rather crooked branches. Most have very restricted ranges in north Florida and prefer moist, fertile soils. Magnolias produce large, showy flowers in the spring, and these develop into fruiting cones that contain numerous reddish seeds, 1/3 to 2/5 inch long, that are eaten by birds and other wildlife after they ripen in the fall. Magnolias have only moderate wildlife value, although they frequently are planted for their beauty. The other member of this family, the tulip tree (*Liriodendron tulipifera*), has little wildlife value.

Cucumber magnolia (*Magnolia acuminata*) occurs locally in fertile woodland soils in the central Panhandle. This is one of the largest magnolias and may reach 75 feet in height. The large, oval leaves are deciduous, and the flowers are odorless. Fruit production is dependable annually, but larger crops occur every three to five years.

Ashe magnolia (*M. ashei*) is endemic to Florida and occurs in mixed woodlands of the central and western Panhandle. Generally considered to be a distinct subspecies of the bigleaf magnolia (*M. macrophylla*), which is not native in Florida, Ashe magnolia is a deciduous, understory shrub-tree that rarely exceeds 20 feet in height. Large, fragrant flowers are produced when the plant is just a few feet tall, and the large, shoe-shaped leaves develop shortly after the flowers. This unique plant makes an interesting addition to woodland landscapes within its range, but its small size and relatively open habit greatly reduces its value to wildlife.

Southern magnolia (*M. grandiflora*) is one of the grandest symbols of southern landscapes. This evergreen magnolia often reaches 65 feet in height and has a distinct pyramid shape. The large, leathery leaves enhance its cover value to wildlife, and its adaptability to its growing site allows its use in a variety of conditions, including coastal areas. Although its natural range extends only to south-central Florida, it is grown in cultivation even in southern areas of the state. The large, fragrant flowers produce good fruit crops annually.

Pyramid magnolia (*M. pyramidata*) is a slender, 30- to 45-foot-tall, deciduous tree native to moist woodland soils of the central and western Panhandle. The large leaves are shaped much like the tongue of a shoe and are clustered near the branch tips. The white flowers are fragrant.

Umbrella magnolia (*M. tripetala*) is a 30- to 40-foot-tall, northern deciduous tree found in Florida only on one north-facing wooded bluff in the central Panhandle. Its use in Florida is greatly limited by its growing requirements. It has large, oval leaves and small, strong-scented flowers that may be overwhelming at close distance.

Sweet bay (*M. virginiana*) has the greatest natural distribution of the Florida magnolias, occurring throughout the state in moist habitats except the Keys. It is an attractive tree, 60 to 70 feet tall, with medium-sized, elliptical, evergreen leaves; smooth, whitish bark; and a narrow crown. The undersides of the leaves are silvery pubescent, and this adds to its beauty whenever a breeze blows. Leaves have a baylike fragrance when crushed and may be used in cooking. Although it naturally occurs in moist soil habitats, it is adaptable to drier sites in cultivation. One drawback is its tendency to produce roots at the soil surface that may sucker if disturbed. Because of its narrow crown and relatively open nature, sweet bay is not especially valuable for wildlife cover, but it serves as a larval food plant for tiger swallowtail butterflies.

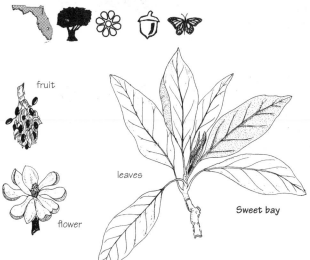

fruit

leaves

flower

Sweet bay

Malpighiaceae (Malpighia family)

The malpighias are a moderate-sized family of trees, shrubs, and vines native to tropical regions of the world. The flowers and fruits of many species are often showy, and some are cultivated as ornamentals in greenhouses or in warm climates. The Barbados-cherry (*Malpighia glabra*) is commonly grown in south Florida for its red fleshy fruits. Members of this family are characterized by simple, evergreen leaves, and flowers in racemes with hooded, clawed petals. All plants in this family are monoecious.

Locust-berry/Key byrsonima (*Byrsonima lucida*) is a broad-crowned, irregular shrub (to about 15 feet) native to the pine rockland forests of the Keys. Its short thin branches can be identified by the prominent joints on the twigs. Many white or pink flowers are produced mostly in the spring. The blooms typically change color to yellow or rose-red after several days. Numerous 1/4-inch fruits, similar to tiny peaches, ripen to red by summer and are eagerly consumed by birds and other wildlife. Locust-berry is an attractive landscape addition, but its use is restricted to areas of Florida where cold temperatures are not normally encountered. Birds are not likely to nest in its spindly branches, but its dense foliage provides good concealment, and its value as a food plant add to its overall usefulness.

Moraceae (Mulberry family)

This family is represented by two genera in Florida with good wildlife value—the mulberries (*Morus* spp.) and the figs (*Ficus* spp.). Both produce abundant crops of sweet, succulent fruit that are eagerly sought by wildlife. Because they are bird-dispersed, they tend to rapidly colonize disturbed openings in woodland habitats. Figs serve as the larval food plant for one of south Florida's most beautiful butterflies, the ruddy daggerwing.

Strangler fig (*Ficus aurea*) is a native of south Florida hammock woodlands. The sticky seeds lodge in the branches of other trees, germinate, and then grow rapidly downward with aerial roots. When these roots reach the soil, the fig begins to engulf its host, eventually smothering it. Strangler fig has thick, elliptical, evergreen leaves that provide cover.

Flowering and fruit production occurs nearly year-round. The rounded fruits are about 3/4 of an inch in diameter.

Shortleaf fig (*F. citrifolia*) is less common than strangler fig and is confined to the hammock woodlands of extreme south Florida. It is very similar in habits to its more common relative, differing mostly in its more rounded leaves and in having the fruit attached by short stalks to the stems.

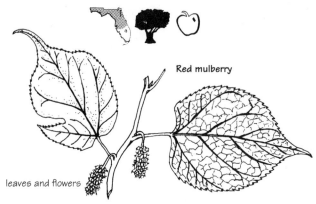

Red mulberry

leaves and flowers

Red mulberry (*Morus rubra*) is a 40- to 50-foot-tall, deciduous and dioecious tree native to most of Florida except the extreme south. It is rather weak and "weedy" and prefers moist, fertile soils, although it will thrive in nearly any noncoastal, upland setting. The broad, spreading crown and numerous branches give it good cover value. Flowering occurs in the spring, and fruits ripen on female trees about two months later. The cylindrical, 1-inch-long, juicy, purple fruits are prized by birds and mammals, but the purple stains caused by their droppings can be a nuisance to humans. Mulberries also provide for many small, insect-eating birds in the spring, because their numerous flowers attract a wealth of pollinating insects. Although mulberries are excellent plants for wildlife, their spreading growth habit and the staining potential of their fruit should be considered prior to planting, so that neighbors won't be offended.

Myricaceae (Wax myrtle family)

The wax myrtles (*Myrica* spp.) in Florida are a family of dioecious, evergreen shrubs with fairly simple, elliptical leaves and small waxy fruit. They are a valuable group of plants for several reasons: wax myrtles can grow in poor soils and improve them because their roots contain nitrogen-fixing bacteria, much like legumes; their dense branching and foliage create excellent wildlife cover; and the numerous fruits provide food for many songbirds. The myrtle warbler (now known as the yellow-rumped warbler) was named for its affinity for wax myrtle fruit. The waxy coating on the fruit is the source of bayberry wax, used to scent candles and soaps. The shrubs are not long-lived, however. The small inconspicuous flowers are produced in the spring, and the dry fruits ripen on female plants by late summer or early fall. Three species are native to Florida.

Southern wax myrtle (*Myrica cerifera*) occurs throughout Florida in a variety of habitats. This adaptable, 20- to 30-foot-tall shrub grows from coastal to inland areas on wet to upland sites in full sun to semi-shaded woodlands. The crushed leaves are aromatic. Southern wax myrtle is excellent as a hedge or thicket, because it responds well to shearing and will sucker if allowed to. A distinct dwarf variety, *M. cerifera* var. *pumila*, occurs that remains at about 3 feet in height. The 1/16-inch fruits are especially attractive to tree swallows and certain warblers.

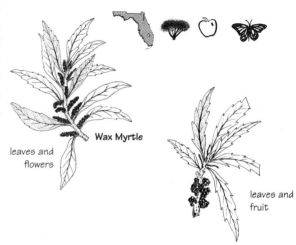

Wax Myrtle

leaves and flowers

leaves and fruit

Swamp bayberry (*M. heterophylla*) is a 9-foot-tall shrub native to wet soil habitats in north and north-central Florida. This bayberry is similar in appearance to southern wax myrtle, but the leaves tend to be slightly larger and more leathery, and the branches are very dark in color.

Odorless wax myrtle (*M. inodora*) is the only Florida native member of this genus with non-aromatic leaves. This 15- to 20-foot-tall shrub occurs mostly in wet soil habitats in the western and central Panhandle. Unlike southern wax myrtle, the leaves are broadly oval, leathery, and normally without teeth near the tips. The fruits also are about twice as large as those of southern wax myrtle, not as numerous, and held away from the stems on noticeable stalks.

Myrsinaceae (Myrsine family)

This is a large tropical family with two members that occur naturally in south and central Florida. Both have broad, oval, evergreen leaves and small round fruits that are eaten mostly by birds and small mammals.

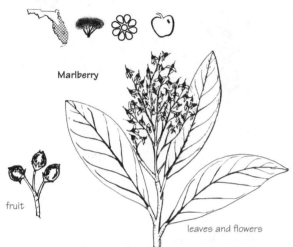

Marlberry

fruit

leaves and flowers

Marlberry (*Ardisia escallonoides*) is a common understory shrub of moist soil habitats. In central Florida, it often does not exceed 3 to 4 feet in height because it is cold sensitive. In south Florida, it may reach 20 feet. Marlberry is an excellent choice for shady, alkaline areas. The numerous richly aromatic, white flowers occur at various times during the year, and these are followed by purple, 1/3-inch-diameter, marblelike fruit. As a thicket, marlberry provides good hiding cover, but the branches are weak and not very good for nesting birds.

Myrsine (*Myrsine guianensis*, syn. *M. floridana, Rapanea punctata, R. guianensis*) is a single-trunked, shrubby tree native to coastal and inland hammock habitats from central to southern Florida. This plant has more tolerance of cold than does marlberry, and can be used along the coast to north-central areas. Myrsine may reach 20 feet in height. It is dioecious, and the inconspicuous flowers appear along the stems in late winter. Round, 1/4-inch, blackish fruits ripen on the female plants in late summer. Myrsine will sucker and form thickets if allowed to. As a thicket, it provides good cover, but the short, thin branches do not encourage bird nesting, and the fruits are only moderately attractive as a food source.

Myrtaceae (Myrtle family)

This is one of the largest families of flowering plants world-wide, with the majority of them being tropical in distribution. All species native to the United States occur in south Florida. These species are small- to medium-sized, evergreen shrubs with simple, often aromatic, leaves and small fleshy fruit. Flowers are white and often fragrant and attractive. All are tolerant of shade, salt, and alkaline soil. Members of this family provide moderate wildlife cover, but birds and other wildlife greatly favor the fruit. Non-native members of this family include Surinam cherry (*Eugenia uniflora*) and the various species of guavas (*Psidium* spp.).

Spicewood (*Calyptranthes pallens*) occurs throughout south Florida and seldom exceeds 20 feet in height. It is an attractive shrub with arching branches tipped with rusty-colored new growth. Clusters of small, non-showy flowers bloom in early summer, and the reddish, 1/4-inch fruits ripen to black by fall. These are consumed mostly by birds. Spicewood grows best in partial shade in moist soil.

Myrtle-of-the-river (*C. zuzygium*) is similar in most respects to spicewood, but it is less common and occurs naturally only in extreme south Florida. The leaves differ by being a rather dull greenish yellow, and larger plants may reach 40 feet in height. The ripe fruits are about 1/3 of an inch in diameter.

STOPPERS (*Eugenia* spp.) are so named because their leaves were used by early settlers as a remedy for diarrhea. They are a common component of the understory of south Florida coastal and hardwood hammocks, because they are adaptable and because their great fruit production is widely dispersed in the droppings of birds. Four species are native to Florida. All produce rather large numbers of attractive, small white flowers that enhance their landscape value.

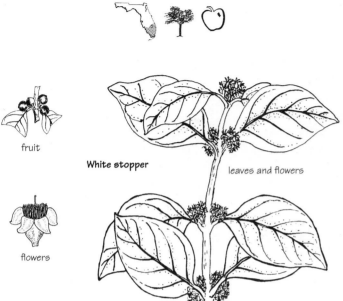

fruit

White stopper

flowers

leaves and flowers

White stopper (*Eugenia axillaris*) is the most widely distributed native stopper, occurring well into central Florida along the coast. Named for its light-colored bark, it may reach 25 feet in height. New growth is reddish, and the leaves are pointed. Flowering occurs in summer, and the 1/3-inch, red fruits ripen to black by fall. The foliage of this plant is extremely aromatic and smells skunklike. During the heat of the Florida summer, white stopper often can be detected by smell before it is seen.

Red-berry stopper (*E. confusa*) is a 20- to 30-foot-tall, shrubby tree native to the coastal hammocks of extreme south Florida. Like white stopper, new growth is reddish and the leaves are pointed. The foliage is not so aromatic, however, and flowering occurs mostly in the fall. Ripe fruit is brilliant red in late winter and about 1/4 of an inch in diameter.

Spanish stopper (*E. foetida*) is a 15- to 20-foot-tall shrubby tree with rather small, rounded, aromatic leaves. Although its scientific name suggests that the foliage smells awful, I have not found it to be nearly as strong as white stopper. Flowering occurs in the summer, and the 1/4-inch, blackish fruits ripen by late fall. Spanish stopper is attractive, but its thin branches do not provide good nesting cover for most birds.

Red stopper (*E. rhombea*) is currently listed as an endangered species and is found in Florida only in the Keys. This shrubby tree generally grows to 15 to 20 feet in height. The large, oval, pointed leaves and smooth, light gray bark give this attractive plant a distinctive look. Flowering occurs in the spring, and the 1/4-inch fruits ripen to black by late fall.

Simpson stopper/twinberry stopper (*Myrcianthes fragrans*) is a shrubby tree that may reach 20 feet tall in shady south Florida hammocks, but usually is about half that size when grown in sunny locations. This plant has the greatest distribution in Florida of any myrtle family member, and it can be grown in nearly any upland location, coastal to inland, in central and south Florida. The small rounded leaves and flaky reddish bark are distinctive. The rather stiff branches give this species better overall cover and nesting value for wildlife than its relatives. Fragrant white flowers are produced on long stalks in spring across the whole crown of the plant. The bright red, 1/3-inch fruits ripen by summer and are very quickly eaten by birds.

Long-stalked stopper (*Psidium longipes*) is a rather common, but unnoticed, many-branched, straggling shrub (sometimes upright) native to the pinelands of south Florida. Florida's only native guava, this plant produces edible, 1/4-inch, black fruits on long stalks, which are readily eaten by wildlife. Its value as a cover plant, however, is minimal. Flowering occurs in spring and the fruits ripen by fall.

Nyctaginaceae (Four-o'clock family)

This is a family mostly of the American tropics that includes a number of widely used annual and perennial flowers, including four o'clocks and bougainvillea. Only one native woody species has value as a food and cover plant for wildlife.

Blolly (*Guapira discolor*) is a 30- to 40-foot-tall tree native to coastal woodlands throughout south Florida. It is broad crowned, and the thick, oval, evergreen leaves enhance its cover value for birds and other wildlife. The rather weak branches are of only moderate value to nesting birds, however. Blolly is dioecious, but my two male trees

produce a few female flowers and fruits each year. Numerous small, green, tubular flowers are produced from late spring throughout the summer, and many clusters of 1/3-inch, bright red fruits develop on female trees. Although extremely showy, the fruits are eaten quickly by birds. A small cluster of blolly used in either a sunny location or the edge of a woodland canopy would be an effective wildlife landscape choice for south Florida homeowners.

Nyssaceae (Tupelo family)

This is a very small family of woody plants found only in eastern North America and China. Closely related to dogwoods, Florida's native tupelos have small, dense clusters of non-showy, fragrant flowers in the spring and clusters of rather large fruits that dangle away from the stems on stalks and ripen by fall. All three species of tupelo in North America belong to the same genus (*Nyssa* spp.) and occur naturally in Florida. They are important bee trees and are the source of tupelo honey.

Water tupelo (*Nyssa aquatica*) is a large (to 100 feet) tree, resident to cypress swamps and bottomland forests in north Florida. The tall, straight trunk often has a broad, spreading base. The narrow, rounded crown and strong branches provide good cover and nesting sites. The 3- to 4-inch-wide, oval leaves often have slightly toothed margins, and they turn a brilliant red in the fall. Water tupelo produces clusters of both male and female flowers on the same tree. The purple fruits, 1 to 1 1/2 inches in length, are produced in abundance each fall and are used by many wildlife.

Ogeechee lime (*N. ogeche*) is a shrubby tree (to about 50 feet in height) found primarily along river swamps in north Florida. Its numerous erect branches and oval, 4- to 6-inch leaves provide good nesting and hiding cover for many wildlife. Its vivid fall color, ranging from purplish to scarlet, makes it aesthetically attractive. Ogeechee lime is dioecious. The large, 1 1/2-inch-long, bright red, acidic fruits ripen by summer and can be used as a lime substitute or made into preserves. Some mammals and birds also eat them.

Black gum (*N. sylvatica*) is a large tree (to 120 feet) widely distributed from north to south-central Florida in moist and bottomland forest habitats. Two forms generally are recognized: *N. sylvatica* var. *sylvatica* occurs in more upland sites in north Florida, while *N. sylvatica* var. *biflora* is largely a bottomland forest resident. From a wildlife standpoint, the trees are otherwise similar and are excellent additions to the landscape. This long-lived tree is rather adaptable and can do well in a variety of non-coastal sites once established. Similar in shape and cover value to water tupelo, the oval-shaped leaves lack any teeth to the margins and turn brilliant red in the fall, even in central Florida. Black gum is dioecious. The spring flowers form 1/2-inch, dark blue fruits by fall that are a favorite wildlife food.

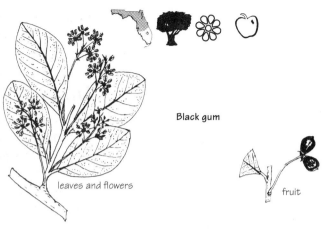

Black gum

leaves and flowers

fruit

Olacaceae (Tallowwood family)

This is a small family of mostly tropical plants represented by two species in Florida. Both of these are evergreen shrubs that often parasitize the roots of neighboring plants, using them to help with water and nutrient intake but not seriously harming them. Flowering and fruit production extends for many months during the year. The fruit are eaten by wildlife, but are not an important food source.

Gray twig (Schoepfia chrysophylloides) is an uncommon, 10- to 15-foot-tall shrub found in extreme south Florida, mostly in the Keys. Its thin grayish branches do not provide much wildlife cover. Small, aromatic, reddish flowers that form along the stems, however, produce 1/2-inch, fleshy fruits that are eaten by birds.

Hog plum/tallowwood (Ximenia americana) is a thorny, often sprawling, shrub found in sandy coastal and inland habitats from northeast Florida through the Keys. Its crooked, dense, and spiny branches and dense leaves give it good cover value to wildlife. Mature yellow fruits are rounded, about 1 inch in diameter, juicy, and very acidic. The flesh and the kernels are edible and used by some wildlife, mostly mammals and larger

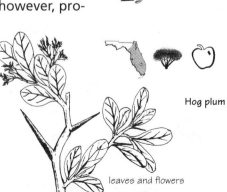

Hog plum

leaves and flowers

birds. The fruits contain hydrocyanic acid, and eating large quantities of it can cause toxic reactions in people.

Oleaceae (Olive family)

This medium-sized family is composed of both tropical and temperate trees and shrubs, including the true olive (*Olea europaea*) and commonly used ornamentals such as ligustrum. Four genera are native to Florida. Florida's olive family members have opposite leaves and are dioecious. All, except the ashes (*Fraxinus* spp.), produce fruits that are berrylike surrounding a stony pit. Ashes produce a flattened, winged seed, somewhat similar to the maples (*Acer* spp.).

Pygmy fringe tree (*Chionanthus pygmaeus*) is an endangered, dwarf version of the more common fringe tree discussed in detail below, and its wildlife value is similar. Endemic to well-drained, sandy habitats in central Florida, this shrubby tree rarely exceeds 8 feet in height. Its small size and rather open character limits its value as wildlife cover. Pygmy fringe tree blooms and bears fruit within two years of age, when it stands barely over 1 foot in height. Given good drainage and a mostly sunny location, this beautiful tree is otherwise adaptable.

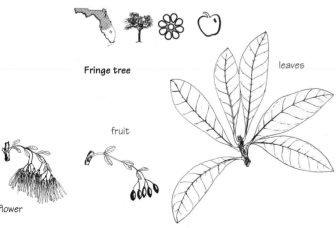

Fringe tree

leaves

fruit

flower

Fringe tree (*Chionanthus virginicus*) is a slow-growing, often multi-trunked, 15- to 20-foot-tall, deciduous tree native to north and central Florida. It prefers fertile, moist soil and seems to perform best when placed at the edge of a wooded canopy. Soil and light conditions become especially important at the southern edge of its range. Fringe trees have rather large, oval leaves that are mostly confined to the tips of the branches. It is one of the last trees to leaf out in the spring and one of the first to defoliate in the fall. This, and its open branching pattern, limit its value as wildlife cover. Its common name is derived from its flowers, which have four long, thin petals and which literally cover the tree in the late spring in a fragrant, fringed mantle of white. The 1/2- to 3/4-inch, purple fruits ripen by summer and are eaten by many birds and other wildlife.

PRIVETS (*Forestiera* spp.), sometimes referred to as wild olives, are small-leaved, multi-stemmed shrubs. Rather small flowers are produced in abundance along the stems in late winter or spring. Their strong fragrance is somewhat like overripe fruit, and they attract a diverse variety of pollinating flies, in addition to bees and butterflies. All but the swamp privet (*F. acuminata*) produce small, dark purple fruits that are eagerly consumed by birds. Four species are native to Florida.

Swamp privet (*Forestiera acuminata*) is a deciduous shrub with rather thin, weak branches that may reach 25 to 30 feet in height. As its name suggests, it is resident to wet soil habitats, and it occurs naturally in north and north-central Florida. When used as a thicket in a wetland setting, this shrub provides good escape cover, but its branches are not good nesting cover for most birds. Its wrinkled, 1-inch, pinkish fruits ripen in mid-summer and are eaten by mammals and some larger birds.

Godfrey's privet (*F. godfreyi*) is a deciduous shrub, similar in growth form to swamp privet, but native to moist, alkaline, woodland soils in north and north-central Florida. The leaves are broadly oval with pointed tips, and the stems are pubescent. The 1-inch-long, purple fruits ripen by midsummer.

Flatwoods privet (*F. ligustrina*) is a deciduous shrub native to upland woodland soils in north and north-central Florida. Its small, elliptical leaves and dense, stiff branches provide good wildlife cover, especially when planted in a small grouping. Its small, 1/2-inch, purple fruits, which ripen by midsummer, also are an excellent wildlife food source.

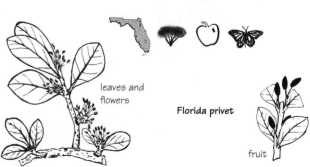

leaves and
flowers

Florida privet

fruit

Florida privet/wild olive (*F. segregata*) is an evergreen shrub of coastal dune and hammock habitats throughout Florida (except the northwest coast) that may reach 20 feet in height. A smaller variant of south Florida pinelands, referred to as pineland privet (*F. pinetorum*), is given separate species status by some taxonomists. Florida privet is an extremely adaptable shrub that will live under a variety of soil and moisture conditions and that can be sheared and kept as a formal hedge. Its stiff, dense branches and many elliptical leaves make it excellent wildlife cover, while the 1/4-inch, purple fruits that ripen in early summer provide food for many birds and small mammals.

ASHES (*Fraxinus* spp.) are medium to large deciduous trees. Their compound leaves are similar in appearance to hickory leaves, but are opposite each other in pairs on the branches. Ashes produce large, rounded canopies that provide cover for wildlife that require overstory foliage. The flattened, winged seeds are used mostly by squirrels, although some birds will feed on them. Four species of ashes occur in Florida.

White ash (*Fraxinus americana*) is a large tree (often to 90 feet) resident to fertile woodland soils in north Florida. Its leaves have a distinctive whitish "bloom" on the underside and usually are composed of seven leaflets. The 1- to 2 1/2-inch seeds ripen by late summer. Good seed crops are produced every two to three years.

Pop ash (*F. caroliniana*) is the smallest ash native to Florida, rarely exceeding 40 feet in height. It is often multi-trunked. Pop ash is widely and commonly distributed in wet soil habitats from north Florida to the edge of the Everglades in the south. It frequently grows with bald cypress trees (*Taxodium* spp.) in standing water. Leaves are composed of five leaflets. Because it is a rather weak tree, it does not provide wildlife cover as well as other members of this genus. Large, dependable crops of 1- to 2-inch seeds are produced annually.

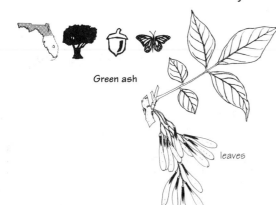

Green ash

leaves

Green ash (*F. pennsylvanica*) is a common component of northern forests, but in Florida it is found mostly in moist to wet forest habitats in the north and north-central regions. In appearance, this tree greatly resembles white ash, one difference being that the undersides of its leaves are greenish. The 1- to 2 1/2-inch seeds are produced in good numbers annually.

Pumpkin ash (*F. profunda*) is a 70- to 80-foot-tall tree resident to wet woodland habitats in north and north-central Florida. Like the tupelos discussed previously, its trunk often has a wide base, and the trees can withstand periodic flooding. Leaves are normally composed of seven broad leaflets. The 2- to 3-inch seeds are produced in good crops annually.

WILD OLIVES / DEVILWOODS (*Osmanthus* spp.) are thick-leaved, evergreen trees with rather open branches and strong, dense wood. Small but aromatic flowers in the spring produce rounded, olivelike fruit in the fall. Wild olives provide some cover, but the rather large and dry fruits are of minimal interest to most wildlife. Two closely related species occur in Florida.

Wild olive (*Osmanthus americanus*) is a 20- to 30-foot tree native to north and central Florida in a wide variety of habitats. Although its best growth occurs in fertile woodland areas, it tolerates deep, infertile sands in coastal and interior sites. The 1/2-inch, purplish fruits are small enough to be used by mammals and most birds.

Scrub olive (*O. megacarpa*) is a 20-foot tree endemic to deep sandy soils in central Florida. In most respects, it closely resembles *O. americanus*, but the fruits are nearly twice as large. This greatly limits their usefulness for birds, and they are eaten mostly by mammals.

Palmae (Palm family)

Palms are not woody plants, but are related to grasses and sedges. Nevertheless, their growth form is treelike or shrublike, and they provide similar functions in the ecosystems where they reside. Palms are characterized by the stiff, evergreen fronds clustered near their growing tips. This foliage provides excellent cover for many species of wildlife. Palms also produce large amounts of rounded fruits composed of a fleshy exterior surrounding a hard inner nut. Palm fruits are eaten by many birds and small mammals. The clusters of small, white, aromatic flowers attract bees and many other pollinating insects.

Paurotis palm (*Acoelorrhaphe wrightii*) is a slender, 20- to 30-foot-tall tree that grows as a multi-trunked clump. Although it naturally occurs in brackish wetland areas of south Florida, it is quite adaptable to upland locations, and it has some cold tolerance. The large, fan-shaped leaves, armed with stout curved spines along the stem, and the density of the foliage created by its clumping nature create excellent wildlife cover. Numerous 1/4-inch, black fruits ripen mostly in the late fall and provide a food source for many species of wildlife.

Silver thatch palm (*Coccothrinax argentata*) is a small (to about 20 feet), single-trunked palm native to the alkaline pinelands of south Florida. This palm has little cold tolerance. The deeply divided, fan-shaped leaves are silvery below, giving it an attractive appearance in a light breeze. The leaf stems are without spines. Because of its small stature and relatively open crown, this is not one of the better palms for wildlife cover. The numerous 1/2-inch, reddish purple to black fruits are sweeter than most palms, however, and provide a good wildlife food source. The fruits are ripe mostly in the fall.

Sargent's cherry palm/buccaneer palm (*Pseudophoenix sargentii*) is Florida's rarest native palm and currently is classified as an endangered species. Its present range in Florida is confined to the northern Keys, but it could be used in upland sites throughout extreme south Florida. This is a very slow-growing, single-trunked tree that rarely exceeds 20 feet in height. The large (up to 10 feet long), featherlike fronds have no spines on the stem and form a broad, spreading crown that is not very good wildlife cover. The numerous 3/4-inch, cherry-red fruits are used by medium-sized and larger birds and many mammals.

Needle palm (*Rhapidophyllum hystrix*) is a slow-growing, ground cover palm that rarely exceeds 6 feet in height. Resident to the shady understory of moist woodlands in north and central Florida, this palm is adaptable and has fared well even in parking lot plantings. The leaves are deeply dissected and fan shaped. When the fronds die and slough off, they leave long, slender, and very sharply pointed needles at the base of each stem. Therefore, groupings of these palms can provide excellent low cover for wildlife. Needle palms are dioecious. The 1/3-inch, reddish brown fruits, which ripen in the fall, are used by some wildlife.

Florida royal palm (*Roystonea elata*) is one of the most ornamentally attractive land-  scape palms. With its tall (to 130 feet), columnar, light gray trunk, its bright green shaft near the crown, and its large (to 13 feet), dark green, featherlike leaves, this palm is visually stunning. It is not one of the best palms, however, for wildlife value. Because the long stiff leaves fall away from the crown in a rather loose arrangement, they provide little cover for most wildlife. Fruit production is seasonal, and the 1/2-inch, bluish black berries ripen in the summer. Their large size limits their use to mammals and larger birds. Florida royal palm is very rare in the wild, but it is used in the landscape as far north as south-central Florida.

Scrub palmetto (*Sabal etonia*) is essentially a trunkless, 4-foot-tall cabbage palm, en-  demic to the well-drained sands of coastal and interior north to south-central Florida. Its fan-shaped leaves are relatively few in number and yellowish green. There are no spines on the leaf stem. Although this is not the showiest native palm, scrub palmetto makes a good wildlife ground cover for sunny and sandy locations. The 1/2-inch, blackish fruits, which ripen in the summer, are eaten by some wildlife.

Dwarf palmetto (*Sabal minor*) is another trunkless cabbage palm relative. This 6- to 9-  foot-tall shrub occurs mostly in the shady understory of moist woodlands in north central Florida. The fan-shaped leaves are bluish green and without spines on the stem. When planted in masses in shady locations, dwarf palmetto can be both attractive and a valuable wildlife cover plant. The 1/3-inch, black fruits, which ripen in late fall, also are useful to many wildlife.

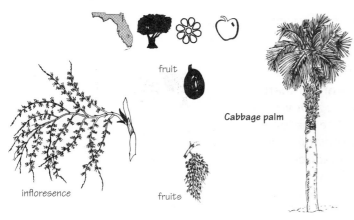

fruit

Cabbage palm

infloresence

fruits

Cabbage palm/sabal palm (*Sabal palmetto*), Florida's state tree, occurs throughout Florida in coastal and inland sites. Its best growth occurs in moist, fertile hammock soils, but it is extremely adaptable. The cabbage palm also is one of the best palms for wildlife. Often 60 to 80 feet tall, the dense, rounded crown of fan-shaped leaves provides excellent hiding and nesting cover. Numerous 1/3-inch, black fruits ripen in the fall. They are sweeter than most palms and are widely used by wildlife.

Saw palmetto (*Serenoa repens*) is both the symbol of the Florida Native Plant Society and of the Florida landscape in general. This plant occurs nearly everywhere in Florida, and grows in nearly every conceivable soil, water, and light condition. We have not valued this hardy and attractive plant in the landscape, perhaps because it is so common. Often nearly trunkless and 4 to 6 feet tall, it will sometimes develop noticeable trunks (especially in very wet soils) and grow to 20 feet in height. The dense leaves with small, sawlike teeth along the stem produce excellent cover for wildlife. Fleshy, 3/4-inch, black fruits ripen in the late summer and are used mostly by mammals. A distinct form of this plant with silvery blue leaves occurs along Florida's east coast.

Brittle thatch palm (*Thrinax morrisii*) is a rare, small (20 to 30 feet tall), single-trunked palm native to the Florida Keys. The deeply dissected, fan-shaped, shiny green leaves with silvery undersides form a small, rounded, open crown that is of only marginal value to wildlife as cover. The numerous small (1/8- to 1/4-inch), white fruits ripen in the fall and are used by many birds and mammals.

Florida thatch palm (*Thrinax radiata*) is slightly taller than brittle thatch palm and occurs in extreme south Florida in addition to the Keys. Its leaves also are more yellowish green and are not silvery beneath. In other respects it is very similar, and its wildlife value is basically identical.

Pinaceae (Pine family)

If any group of plants characterizes natural Florida, it is the pines (*Pinus* spp.). Many of Florida's most widespread ecosystems are dominated by pines. Thus, the state has slash pine flatwoods, longleaf pine sandhills, and sand pine scrubs. Pines grow throughout Florida and occur in most habitats. Their wide-spreading crowns, strong limbs, and ever-green needles provide excellent wildlife cover. Even after they die, pines are a favored nesting tree for many species of animals. Pine seeds, usually 1/4 inch to 1/2 inch long, are quite nutritious and are eaten by many birds and small mammals. Some animals even will chew the cones to get at the seeds before they open. Others, including the birds, must wait until the cones ripen and the seeds are exposed. Like the oaks, pines vary in the amount of seed produced, and some skip years between good seed crops. Cones ripen the second year after they form, and the seeds generally are dispersed in the fall.

Sand pine (*Pinus clausa*) is a medium-sized tree (rarely exceeding 70 feet) native to deep, well-drained, sandy habitats of north and central Florida. The 2- to 3 1/2-inch-long, slender needles occur in bundles of two and give the tree a kind of feathery appearance. Sand pines grow quickly, but generally are not long lived. The cones persist on the tree, often for many years, and many of them remain closed until after a fire. This allows it to colonize burned areas quickly, but it reduces its value as a wildlife food tree.

Shortleaf pine (*P. echinata*) is another medium-sized pine with relatively short needles. Its distribution is limited in Florida to upland areas in the Panhandle, however, and the 3- to 5-inch-long, flexible needles come in bundles of two or three. This is a fast-growing tree and has the smallest cones of any of Florida's native pines. Seed production is heavy and they are well-used by wildlife.

Slash pine (*P. elliottii*) is the state's most widely distributed pine, occurring statewide in a variety of habitats. Its name is derived from the practices of the turpentine industry, once vitally important to the state's economy. The tree trunks were slashed and the dripping sap was collected to be distilled into turpentine. Slash pines produced more sap than any other pine. These trees also produce large and regular seed crops that are important

wildlife food. Their 5- to 11-inch-long, rigid needles in bundles of two or three provide good cover. Slash pines are drought tolerant and well-adapted to all but the most excessively drained, sandy Florida soils. They can also tolerate periodic flooding for short duration and are relatively salt tolerant. Two varieties occur in Florida: *P. elliottii* var. *elliottii*, occurring in north and central Florida, has an open, irregular crown; *P. elliottii* var. *densa* occurs in central and south Florida and has a more rounded crown, denser needles, and slower growth rate. "Improved" strains of the former, promoted by some agencies, are good for quick timber production, but their lack of branches greatly limits their wildlife cover value.

Spruce pine (*P. glabra*) is a fast-growing, rather large (to 110 feet) tree native to upland woodland soil in north and north-central Florida. Its name is derived from its distinctive nonflaky bark that looks similar to that of the spruces (*Picea* spp). Spruce pine has a rather narrow, open crown and short (2- to 3-inch), slender needles in clusters of two. It does not produce as much wildlife cover as most native pines, but it is one of the most beautiful. The cones are small, but seed production is regular.

Longleaf pine (*P. palustris*) is a large (to 120 feet), long-lived tree found in a variety of upland habitats from north to south-central Florida. As its name implies, its needles (in clusters of three) are extremely long—up to 15 inches and more in length. These are mostly clustered at the tips of the branches and add to its distinctive appearance. The stout branches and long, dense, needles make it an excellent wildlife cover tree, and its relatively flat crown provides a good platform for nesting raptors and wading birds. Longleaf pine also produces the largest cones of any native pine, and the seeds are an important source of wildlife food. Good cone production only occurs every three to four years, however. Longleaf pine often is considered to be slow growing, because it devotes most of its energy during its first three to seven years developing a long taproot. Once this is accomplished, its rate of upward growth is quick. Specimens should be planted at an early age so that their taproots can go downward. Pot-bound trees with taproots coiled in spirals around the bottom of the pot will not develop stable root systems unless the roots are pruned back cleanly and then

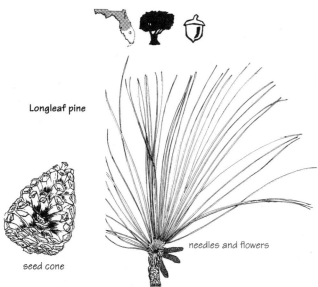

Longleaf pine

seed cone

needles and flowers

forced to redevelop. Longleaf pine is very adaptable to growing conditions (although it prefers well-drained soil) and it has good salt tolerance.

Pond pine (*P. serotina*) is a 50- to 60-foot-tall tree native to north and central Florida. As its name implies, it occurs around ponds and other poorly drained, moist soil habitats. It generally also is a rather crooked tree with an irregular crown. The 4- to 8-inch-long needles normally are in bundles of three. Unique to this pine is its tendency to form sucker sprouts of needles on the trunk and major branches. The 3- to 4-inch-long cones are somewhat spiny and often persist on the tree well after the seeds are shed, sometimes becoming imbedded in the bark of the growing branches. The seeds are not shed for several years after the cones ripen, but they are valuable to wildlife. This is the best pine for use around wetlands or where soils are frequently flooded.

Loblolly pine (*P. taeda*) is Florida's largest pine, often reaching 120 feet in height. It is quick to establish itself in disturbed sites and is sometimes referred to as oldfield pine because of this. Loblolly pine is native to fertile soil habitats in north and north-central Florida, although it is sometimes planted successfully in south-central regions. When young, this pine somewhat resembles the slash pine, but the loblolly has shorter needles, always with three per sheath. As it matures, it can be further identified by its large, straight trunk and spiny cones. This is an adaptable tree that produces large seed crops and good cover for wildlife. It is more susceptible than other pines, however, to damage from southern pine beetles and fusiform rust disease, which may manifest itself more in urban areas where additional stresses occur or in the southern edge of its range where winters are too mild to kill the disease.

Polygonaceae (Buckwheat family)

This is a large family that includes many species of herbaceous weeds in Florida, but only two species of native trees in one genus: *Coccoloba*. Both species are subtropical and are restricted to south-central and south Florida. Their large, rounded, evergreen leaves provide good cover, their racemes of flowers attract many pollinating insects, and their grape-like fruits, produced in long clusters, are used by many species of wildlife. Both of these species are dioecious.

Pigeon plum (*Coccoloba diversifolia*) is a 30- to 50-foot-tall tree with a stout, straight trunk and a rounded crown. Its dense, thick branches provide excellent nesting cover for birds. Flowering occurs in the spring, and the 1/4-inch, purple fruits ripen by early fall. These are juicy and acidic and sometimes are used in jelly or wine. They are especially attractive to the threatened white-crowned pigeons of extreme south Florida (hence, its name), and many other birds and small mammals. Pigeon plum is native to upland coastal hammocks in south Florida.

Sea grape (*C. uvifera*) is widely planted in landscapes—a shrubby tree that grows naturally on coastal dunes from south-central Florida southward. Because it will suffer damage from below-freezing temperatures, it does not reach its potential size at the northern edge of its range. In south Florida, however, it can reach 25 feet in height, but has a rather short main trunk and gnarled, irregular branches. Sea grape provides valuable wildlife cover to birds and other wildlife in coastal dune habitats. The large racemes of fragrant flowers bloom most abundantly in the spring, but some are produced nearly year-round. Showy clusters of juicy, reddish purple fruits, 3/4 to 1 inch in diameter, are most abundant in late summer. The size of the fruits limit their use to mammals and larger songbirds. The fruits are sometimes used to make jelly.

Rhamnaceae (Buckthorn family)

This is a moderate-sized family that contains a rather diverse variety of native trees and shrubs. Some members have economic importance because of dyes extracted from them or because of their medicinal qualities. Others have showy flowers and have been used horticulturally. Many are important wildlife food producers, developing large numbers of small, juicy, berrylike fruits annually. Few native species, however, become large enough to provide significant value as cover.

Black ironwood

leaves and fruit

Black ironwood (*Krugiodendron ferreum*) is a 30-foot-tall, evergreen tree native to coastal hammocks of south Florida. It has some cold tolerance and can be used in south-central locations where it is somewhat protected. This tree has the distinction of having the densest wood of any

North American plant. This, and its dark, furrowed bark, give it its common name. Black ironwood has a rather narrow crown, but its dense branches provide good wildlife cover. Its leaves are oval, dark shiny green, and about two inches long. The inconspicuous flowers are produced mainly during the summer. The 1/3-inch-diameter, sweet and juicy, black fruits ripen by winter and are especially attractive to birds.

Darling plum (*Reynosia septentrionalis*) is another heavy-wooded, evergreen buckthorn native to coastal hammocks of south Florida. Darling plum is a shrubby tree that may reach 30 feet, but usually is about 20 feet tall. The reddish brown bark becomes scaly with age. The leaves are shiny, deep green, leathery, and oval-shaped. New growth is reddish. Mature specimens provide good escape cover and some nesting cover. Flowering occurs in spring and early summer. Plum-shaped, sweet, juicy, 1/2- to 3/4-inch, purplish fruits ripen by fall. These are quite attractive to birds and other wildlife.

Carolina buckthorn (*Rhamnus caroliniana*) is a 20- to 30-foot-tall, deciduous, shrubby tree native to fertile woodland habitats in north and central Florida. Its open, airy character is attractive, but provides little cover value to wildlife. Numerous greenish white flowers in May produce large crops of 1/3-inch-diameter berries that ripen from red to black by October. The fruits are sweet and very attractive to wildlife. Carolina buckthorn does best in fertile soil of average moisture where it receives about four hours of sun daily. It is quite tolerant of alkaline soil. The dark green, 3- to 4-inch, elliptical leaves turn a rich yellow in the fall.

Buckthorn (*Sageretia minutiflora*) is a slender, often sprawling, deciduous shrub that rarely exceeds 9 feet in height. Native to alkaline, well-drained habitats of north and central Florida, it also has good salt tolerance. This plant behaves more as a ground cover than an upright shrub. The thorny branches tend to creep along the ground, providing little cover for most wildlife. Small, fragrant, white flowers, which bloom in spikes at the branch tips in spring, produce numerous 1/4-inch, purplish fruits that ripen in fall. They are eaten by a variety of wildlife.

Florida jujube (*Ziziphus celata*) is one of the rarest plants native to Florida. After having been "lost" for nearly 50 years, it was rediscovered and described in 1990, and much of its biology is not yet well known. It is a densely branched, thorny shrub with small, round, deciduous leaves. Found only in a few localized populations in certain Highlands County scrubs, it likely would adapt to other central Florida well-drained sandy habitats. Its growth form should make it good for wildlife cover, especially for many nesting birds. The small purple fruits it produces in the fall likely are eaten by birds and small mammals.

Rosaceae (Rose family)

Plants in the rose family are especially abundant in North America and contain some of the most beautiful and wildlife-useful species available for the landscape. Many non-native species are extremely important landscape plants, but surprisingly few natives are grown and cultivated in Florida. Besides the roses, this group includes many important fruit crops including apples, peaches, plums, pears, and cherries, and ornamentals such as the flowering crabapples. Members of this family are characterized by flowers with five showy white, pink, or red petals. Fruits often are abundant, fleshy, and very attractive to a wide variety of wildlife. Many species are either thorny or have short spur branches that are thornlike. This characteristic gives them good value as wildlife cover, especially for many nesting songbirds. Most species are deciduous. Plants in the rose family also are notoriously attractive to wildlife that browse on young twigs, such as rabbits and deer. Young plants may have to be protected if these animals are common in your area.

Downy serviceberry (*Amelanchier arborea*) is a 20- to 30-foot-tall, deciduous tree found in moist, sandy woodlands in areas of the Panhandle. This beautiful narrow-crowned tree blooms profusely in spring with showy, long-petalled white flowers. Numerous sweet, 1/4-inch, violet, blueberrylike fruits ripen by summer and attract every fruit-eating animal imaginable. The young twigs and the oval, slightly-toothed leaves have a downy pubescence. Serviceberry is without any degree of thorniness. It is best planted in north Florida in fertile, well-drained locations where it receives filtered or partial sun.

Red chokeberry (*Aronia arbutifolia*) is a multi-stemmed, 6- to 9-foot-tall, deciduous shrub native to wet and moist soil habitats in north and central Florida. This plant commonly spreads by underground suckers and will form a colony over time, if allowed to. Such colonies provide hiding cover, but the poorly branched stems do not create much cover for nesting wildlife. The major wildlife value of this shrub is the large number of 1/4-inch, deep red, applelike fruits that ripen in the fall and persist well into winter. These develop in small clusters all along the stems and are eaten by many species of wildlife. Numerous white or pinkish white flowers bloom in early spring and the foliage turns crimson red in the fall. Both characteristics add to its ornamental value. Red chokeberry is an excellent selection for the edge of ponds or other moist soil areas, either in sunny or partially sunny locations where its suckering nature will not be a problem.

HAWTHORNS (*Crataegus* spp.). Let me initially confess that I think hawthorns are one of the most useful and beautiful groups of native small trees available for use in north and central Florida. I shamelessly promote them whenever I speak at public meetings, but they are as yet still largely unavailable from the nursery trade. Hawthorns are small (generally 20 to 30 feet tall), deciduous trees that bloom profusely in the spring much like the flowering crabapples. They produce applelike fruit, known as haws, that are a valued wildlife food. Ripe haws are rich in vitamin C and can be used to make jelly. Most hawthorns also are thorny, but the degree of thorniness varies both within and among species. They are excellent cover choices for many nesting birds and other wildlife. Hawthorns give plant taxonomists a fit, because even the recognized species vary greatly in characteristics such as leaf shape, and hybridization frequently occurs. Some taxonomists have described more than 700 species in North America, while others have condensed the number to several dozen. I will describe the ten species that are both distinct and generally accepted as Florida natives.

Mayhaw (*Crataegus aestivalis*) is a 20- to 25-foot-tall tree with a somewhat crooked, gray-barked trunk and narrow crown. The leaves generally are small, oval, and slightly toothed, although some leaves are lobed. Mayhaw often is armed with straight spines 1/2 to 3/4 of an inch in length. The white to pinkish white flowers occur singly or in groups of two or three. The 1/3-inch, bright red fruits ripen in early summer. These fruits are prized for jelly-making, and a small commercial business has developed around them. Mayhaw is native to wet and moist woodlands of north and north-central Florida, but it is adaptable to average soils once established, and it can be grown throughout central Florida. Use it in filtered sun or partly sunny locations.

Cockspur haw/Wakulla haw (*C. crus-galli,* syn. *C. pyracanthoides*) is a 25- to 30-foot-tall tree with dark, scaly bark and a rather broad crown with widely spreading branches. The small, oval leaves are only slightly toothed along the margins and are quite shiny and deep green in color. As the name suggests, it is armed with stout, straight spines that may be 1 1/2 inches in length. White to pinkish flowers occur in numerous clusters in the spring. The small (about 1/3- inch-long) fruits, which occur in clusters, ripen by summer. Their color ranges from dull red to rusty orange or greenish, and they frequently are mottled with blackish spots. This adaptable hawthorn is native mostly to upland alkaline sites in north and north-central Florida.

Summer haw/yellow haw (*C. flava,* syn. *C. floridana, C. lacrimata*) is a widely occurring and variable, 15- to 20-foot-tall tree of north and central Florida. One of the most picturesque haws, it has a short, crooked trunk and a wide-spreading crown of crooked, sometimes weeping, branches. The toothed leaves are broad and spatula-shaped, and are sometimes lobed. Thorniness is variable, with some specimens being thornless. The thorns, when present, normally are stout, but short (1/4 to 1/2 an inch long). Large white flowers bloom singly or in small clusters in spring. The large (1/2- to 3/4-inch-long), globe-shaped fruit vary in color from greenish yellow to reddish and ripen by summer. This hawthorn is adapted to well-drained, sandy soils and prefers sunny locations.

Scrub haw (*C. lepida*) is not recognized as a species by most taxonomists, yet it is quite distinct. It occurs sporadically in central Florida scrubs and sandhills. Often multi-trunked, the trunks and limbs are exceedingly crooked and arching, and they are armed with stout, straight thorns, 3/4 to 1 inch in length. Unlike other haws, its leaves do not form until late spring. They are similar in shape to summer haw (*C. flava*), but are much smaller in size. Small white flowers bloom in early summer, either singly or in small clusters. The 1/2-inch, orangish red fruits do not ripen until late September or October. Scrub haw requires well-drained sandy soils and prefers full sun.

Parsley haw (*C. marshallii*) is a 20-foot-tall, slender tree native to moist and wet woodlands in north and central Florida. Often multi-trunked, it has rather short crooked branches and a narrow crown. Thorns, when present, are slender and about a 1/2 inch long. The leaves are small with many deeply notched lobes that resemble those of parsley. Numerous clusters of small, white to pinkish white flowers bloom in the spring. Clusters of narrow, bright red, 1/4-inch-long fruits ripen by fall and persist into winter if they are not gobbled up by birds and other wildlife. Parsley haw is a beautiful and delicate tree and is best used in a partly shady, woodland understory. It is adaptable, but may need extra water to get it established.

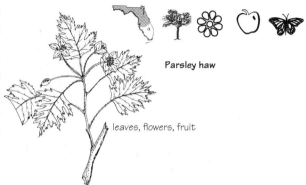

Parsley haw

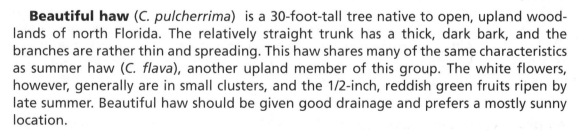

leaves, flowers, fruit

Washington haw (*C. phaenopyrum*) is one of the few hawthorns that has received attention in North America as a landscape plant, but its range in Florida is restricted to the western Panhandle, and this limits its use here. This 20-foot-tall tree has a rather straight trunk with gray bark and broad, spreading branches. The thorns are slender and 1 to 2 inches in length. Washington haw has rather large showy leaves (up to 2 1/2 inches long) that are somewhat maplelike in shape. Clusters of large, showy, white flowers bloom in the spring. The clusters of 1/3-inch, bright red fruits ripen in the fall. This haw also produces some of the best fall color with its scarlet leaves. Within north Florida, Washington haw should be planted in fertile, moist woodland soils in partial sun.

Beautiful haw (*C. pulcherrima*) is a 30-foot-tall tree native to open, upland woodlands of north Florida. The relatively straight trunk has a thick, dark bark, and the branches are rather thin and spreading. This haw shares many of the same characteristics as summer haw (*C. flava*), another upland member of this group. The white flowers, however, generally are in small clusters, and the 1/2-inch, reddish green fruits ripen by late summer. Beautiful haw should be given good drainage and prefers a mostly sunny location.

Littlehip haw (*C. spathulata*) is a 20- to 25-foot-tall tree native to moist woodland habitats of north and north-central Florida. This haw shares some of the same characteristics as parsley haw, but the leaves are linear, sometimes unlobed to deeply lobed, but never sharply toothed. The trees are sometimes thornless. The thorns, when present, are stout, straight, and 1 to 1 1/2 inches long. Often multi-trunked, the outer bark normally peels away in thin plates as the tree matures, revealing an orangish brown inner bark. This adds to the tree's aesthetic character. Numerous clusters of small, white or pinkish white flowers in spring develop into many 1/4-inch-long, cylindrical, bright red fruits in fall. These will persist into winter if they are not eaten first. Littlehip haw is an attractive and valuable wildlife tree that is relatively adaptable, once established.

One-flowered haw (*C. uniflora*) is a shrubby, 10-foot-tall tree native to sandy uplands in north Florida. In many respects it resembles scrub haw. Leaves are roundish and slightly toothed at the outer margins. The branches frequently are armed with slender, straight thorns, 1 to 2 inches in length. As the name suggests, the small flowers are normally produced singly, not in clusters, and the resulting round, reddish, 1/2-inch-long fruits ripen by fall. Because of its small stature, this haw is best planted for wildlife in a grouping to maximize its ability to produce good cover.

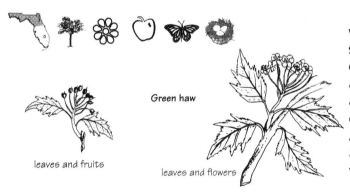

Green haw

leaves and fruits

leaves and flowers

Green haw (*C. viridis*) is a slender, 30-foot-tall tree native to moist and wet soil habitats of north and central Florida. Often largely spineless, the spines, when present, are thin, and 1/2 to 1 inch in length. Green haw is characterized by its wide-spreading branches and rounded crown. Leaves are rather large and triangular in shape with several to many pointed lobes and a noticeably toothed margin. Small, white flowers occur in numerous clusters. The 1/4- to 1/3-inch-long, rounded, orangish red fruits ripen by fall. Although green haw is frequently encountered around wetlands, it will adapt to typical landscape conditions and is both visually attractive and valuable to wildlife.

Southern crabapple (*Malus angustifolia*) is a 30-foot-tall, deciduous tree native to well-drained woodland areas of north Florida. This is the state's only native crabapple, and it is sometimes used in landscapes for its ornamental value. Southern crabapple is a rather stout-trunked tree with a rounded crown. The limbs are frequently armed with short, stiff spines and with spiny spur shoots. In the spring, the trees are covered with pink, aromatic blossoms. The tart, 1-inch-long, greenish crabapples ripen by fall. Although this tree can be successfully grown in central Florida, I do not know of any specimens that have set fruit. Its value as a wildlife plant, therefore, is greatest in north Florida. Southern crabapple will sucker and create a thicket if allowed to. Such thickets are excellent wildlife cover, although even single specimens are good for many nesting birds. This is a short-lived tree, however, and subject to numerous diseases and pests that plague other members of the rose family.

PLUMS AND CHERRIES (*Prunus* spp.) are shrubs or trees recognized by their abundant, showy, white flowers in the spring and their round, juicy fruit surrounding a stone-like inner seed. Plums and cherries are not thorny, but several species of native plums have thornlike spur shoots. Many species sucker and produce dense thickets if permitted to. In addition, the fruits of all species are especially attractive to wildlife and the seeds are widely dispersed in their droppings. In this way, they rapidly colonize open ground. The wilted foliage of cherries is toxic to livestock, so they should not be planted in areas where they might be browsed. Seven species occur naturally in Florida, and members of this group occur statewide and in most habitats.

American plum (*Prunus americana*) is a 20- to 30-foot-tall, deciduous tree native to fertile, often alkaline, areas of north and north-central Florida. This is a shrublike tree with a single short trunk and a dense rounded crown. The branches have numerous thorny spurs. Fragrant white flowers produce 3/4- to 1-inch-diameter, reddish plums that ripen by summer and are useful mostly to mammals. They also make good jelly. American plum is a northern species with a sporadic distribution in Florida. Care should be given to use only Florida stock if you desire to plant this plum. Other native species, with wider Florida distributions may be better choices.

Chickasaw plum (*P. angustifolia*) is one of the toughest and most adaptable members of this genus for use in Florida. Generally a multi-trunked, shrubby, deciduous tree, this 20-foot-tall plum occurs throughout north and central Florida in sandy, well-drained soils, including coastal areas. It suckers frequently and often forms dense thickets that are excellent wildlife cover. Numerous small clusters of white flowers bloom in early spring. The round, reddish to reddish yellow, 1/2-inch plums ripen by early summer. The smaller size of these fruit make them more widely useful to birds than American plum. They, too, are good for jelly.

Cherry laurel (*P. caroliniana*) is an evergreen, narrow-crowned, 30-foot-tall tree native to a variety of habitats in north and central Florida. It has some salt tolerance and occurs inland in both moist and well-drained soils. Cherry laurel is frequently used as a hedge, because it is evergreen and it tolerates regular shearing. It also is sometimes considered a pest, because the seeds are widely distributed by birds and the seedlings rapidly colonize open ground. As a wildlife plant, it is very good at providing both cover and food. Small racemes of white flowers bloom in early spring. The 1/2-inch-long, shiny black fruits ripen by late summer, but will persist into the winter if they are uneaten. Cherry laurel will tolerate a lot of shade if used in a woodland understory, but its best growth occurs in open fertile sites.

Scrub plum (*P. geniculata*) is a 4- to 6-foot-tall, deciduous shrub native only to central Florida scrublands. Its dense, geniculate (zig-zag) branching pattern gives it its species name and creates good wildlife cover for small animals that spend time at or near the ground. Some spur shoots develop, but it is not thorny. As with many plants adapted to hot, arid conditions, the leaves are greatly reduced in size and may drop off during periods of water stress. Tiny white flowers bloom profusely in early spring. These are followed by 1/3-inch-long, sweet, purple plums in early summer. No plum is more eagerly sought by wildlife than these. Scrub plum is an endangered species because of habitat loss. It is reasonably adaptable, however, if planted in sandy soils with good drainage and in mostly sunny locations.

West Indian cherry (*P. myrtifolia*) is a tropical, evergreen, 30-foot-tall tree native to south Florida hammock woodlands. In some respects, it is similar to cherry laurel. The large, glossy leaves have an undulating margin and no teeth. White racemes of flowers bloom in November and December, and the 1/3-inch, black cherries ripen in early summer. West Indian cherry is an adaptable tree and can be used in most south Florida locations, including areas near the coast. As a wildlife plant, it provides both food and cover in good measure.

Black cherry (*P. serotina*) is another species common to eastern North America. In Florida, it occurs in a wide variety of habitats. It is excellent at tolerating the shade of mature woodlands, but it will thrive and rapidly colonize disturbed fields and fence rows. Black cherry is a deciduous, narrow-crowned tree that reaches 100 feet in height. Bark on mature specimens is nearly black. Long racemes of white flowers bloom in the spring. Numerous 1/3-inch, purplish black fruit ripen by summer. Although black cherry produces fruit annually, large crops only occur every three years or so. It also produces good fall color, the leaves turning an orangish red. This is an extremely adaptable and excellent wildlife tree for the northern third of Florida, but—like the cherry laurel—the birds will disperse the seeds widely and seedlings may need to be controlled.

Flatwoods plum (*P. umbellata*) is sometimes called the "forgotten" plum, because it has often been overlooked or ignored. However, it is a beautiful and useful, 15-foot-tall, deciduous tree, and it deserves far more use and recognition. Native to both pine and hardwood woodlands of average drainage in north and central Florida, it may be confused sometimes with chickasaw plum. Differences are many, however. Flatwoods plum is a somewhat crooked, single-trunked tree. The leaf blades are flat, not slightly folded. The white flowers bloom in late spring, several weeks later than chickasaw plum, and the 1/2-inch, red to yellow fruits ripen several weeks later in summer. Flatwoods plum also is not salt tolerant and is less commonly armed with thorny spur shoots. This plum is best used as an understory tree in a woodland landscape where it receives filtered or partial sun.

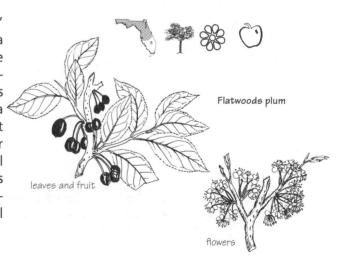

Flatwoods plum

leaves and fruit

flowers

Swamp rose (*Rosa palustris*) is an upright, deciduous, multi-stemmed, six-foot-tall shrub native to wet soil habitats in north and central Florida. Besides the beauty and fragrance of its many single, pink flowers that bloom from spring to early summer, it is a useful wildlife plant. Because each of its numerous stems is armed with a myriad of hooked prickles, it creates a thicket impenetrable to people and most predators, but secure for many small mammals and birds. Its 1/2-inch fruits (hips) also provide food during the winter months. This plant is adaptable, but prefers soils that are constantly moist. It also suckers and will spread if permitted to.

BLACKBERRIES (*Rubus* spp.) are another group of very spiny, deciduous shrubs in the rose family that provide very effective wildlife habitat. Blackberry thickets create excellent cover for rabbits and other small mammals, while the sweet, purple fruit are eagerly eaten by birds and other wildlife. Blackberries flower and fruit on stems that are in their second year of growth. Like the swamp rose, they also will sucker and spread and should not be used in an area where this could be a problem. Four native species occur in Florida.

Highbush blackberry (*Rubus betulifolius*) is an erect shrub that may reach 10 feet in height. It is native to wet woodland habitats in north and central Florida and will tolerate standing water for extended periods of time. Numerous 1/2- to 1-inch-long, flavorful fruits ripen during the summer.

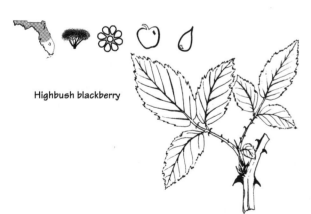

Highbush blackberry

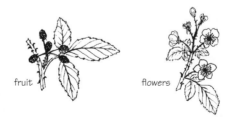

fruit

flowers

Sand blackberry (*R. cuneifolius*) is a drought-tolerant blackberry that commonly forms dense thickets in upland sites, but may occur also in wet areas. The stems often are

arching. Flowers occur singly or in small clusters. The sweet, 1/2- to 1-inch-long fruits ripen in summer. Sand blackberry occurs throughout most of Florida in suitable growing sites.

Northern dewberry (*R. flagellaris*) is a trailing shrub native to open woodlands in the Panhandle. The flowers occur either singly or in small clusters, and the 3/4- to 1-inch fruits ripen in summer. This is the native species from which many commercial varieties of dewberries have been derived. It is at the southern end of its range in north Florida, however, and it is not the best choice for most sites because of that.

Southern dewberry (*R. trivialis*) occurs throughout Florida in a variety of habitats and is the best dewberry for use in the state. Like northern dewberry, it is a trailing shrub that eventually forms an extensive ground cover. Flowers, too, are normally single. The broad sweet fruits are 1/2 to 1 inch long. Southern dewberry grows well in both upland and lowland sites, and is adaptable to most landscape settings.

Rubiaceae (Coffee family)

This is one of the largest families of flowering plants in the world and includes many non-natives that are commercially or horticulturally important, such as the true coffee tree (*Coffea arabis*), gardenia, ixora, and pentas. Members of the coffee family have opposite or whorled leaves that often are elliptical, large, and shiny. The flowers often are bell-shaped and rather showy, while the fruits often are fleshy berries attractive to birds and other wildlife. Most native species are not important cover plants.

Seven-year apple (*Casasia clusiifolia*) is a wide-branching shrub native to south Florida that may reach 20 feet in height. Its pale branches and broad, leathery, spatula-shaped, evergreen leaves, clustered at the branch tips, are distinctive. Most common to coastal dunes in the Keys, it has a high degree of tolerance for both salt and drought, but is not tolerant of freezing temperatures. Seven year apple is dioecious and prefers a sunny location. The flowers of both sexes are white and fragrant, and they bloom during most months. Egg-shaped fruits, two to three inches in length, ripen slowly over a period of

about one year on female plants. Fruit size limits its use mostly to mammals, and its open, branching character reduces its value as wildlife cover.

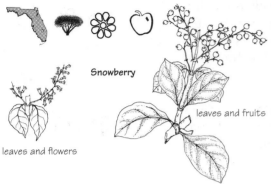

Snowberry

leaves and fruits

leaves and flowers

Snowberry (*Chiococca alba*) is a low, sprawling or erect evergreen shrub native to coastal hammocks throughout much of Florida. Although it may reach about 10 feet in height, its branches most often are almost vinelike as they drape along the ground or clamber among the limbs of neighboring plants. Its value for wildlife cover is minimal, except for use as a ground cover. Snowberry blooms profusely during most months, but particularly in late spring and summer. From the racemes of cream-colored, fragrant flowers develop many clusters of snow-white, 1/4- to 1/2-inch berries. Most ripe fruits are available from late fall through winter. They are not particularly attractive to wildlife as a food source, however.

Pineland snowberry (*Chiococca parviflora*, syn. *C. pinetorum*) is a sprawling shrub very similar to snowberry (*C. alba*), but native only to south Florida pinelands. It is characterized by smaller leaves and fruits. Pineland snowberry should be used as a ground cover for wildlife only in areas that don't normally receive below-freezing temperatures.

Black-torch (*Erithalis fruticosa*) is a many-branched evergreen shrub (to about 8 feet in height) native to extreme south Florida and the Keys. The dense foliage of oval, 1 1/2-inch-long leaves provides excellent hiding cover, especially when planted in mass or with other plant species. The thin branches, however, offer little nesting cover. Numerous clusters of small five-petaled flowers are produced year-round at the leaf axils. The 1/4-inch-diameter, black fruits ripen several months later. They are eaten mostly by birds. Black-torch is another tropical species whose range extends from the Caribbean into Florida. Although a useful and adaptable plant, its sensitivity to cold restricts it to a limited region of the state.

Everglades velvetseed (*Guettarda elliptica*) is a shrubby, 15- to 20-foot-tall tree native to extreme south Florida pinelands and hammocks. The oval, 2-inch-long leaves are smooth on the upper surface. The leaf veins are noticeably indented and give the leaves a wrinkled appearance. Small clusters of yellowish to pinkish white flowers bloom mostly in May or June. They first open in the evening and are fragrant. The 1/3-inch-diameter, rounded, reddish fruits with velvety skins eventually ripen to black by late fall. They are eaten and dispersed mostly by birds.

Roughleaf velvetseed (*G. scabra*) is a common 15- to 20-foot-tall shrubby tree of south Florida pinelands. Its oval, 2- to 6-inch-long, evergreen leaves are both leathery and rough. In other respects, it is quite similar to Everglades velvetseed (*G. elliptica*).

Firebush (*Hamelia patens*) is an evergreen shrub that may reach 15 feet in height in extreme south Florida where freezing temperatures are uncommon. Its range extends, however, to south-central Florida hammocks, and in these locations it generally is much smaller. Firebush is an excellent shrub for areas protected from harsh winter temperatures. The numerous scarlet flowers, which bloom nearly year-round, attract hummingbirds and butterflies, while the large steady crop of 1/4-inch, dark purple fruit attracts many birds and other wildlife. Firebush is tolerant of a wide range of light, moisture, and soil conditions, although it does best in partial sun in fertile, slightly alkaline soil.

WILD COFFEE (*Psychotria* spp.) is a genus of evergreen shrubs related to the true coffees, but not used commercially as a beverage. They are characterized by large, elliptical leaves with noticeably indented veins that give the leaves a wrinkled appearance, as well as many clusters of small, white flowers, followed by clusters of elliptical, 1/4- to 1/3-inch-long, bright red fruit. The flowers can bloom throughout the year, but are most abundant in the spring. They attract some butterflies, particularly the zebra longwing. The fruits ripen mostly in the late fall and winter. Florida's native species are weakly branched and provide cover mostly in the understory. They tolerate dense shade and occur mostly in moist wooded habitats. These three species occur in Florida:

Bahama coffee (*Psychotria ligustrina*) is a 6-foot-tall species native only to south Florida. Leaves of this plant are somewhat wrinkled in appearance, and the flowers and fruit are somewhat smaller than the other species.

Wild coffee (*P. nervosa*) is a variable shrub that occurs from coastal hammocks in northeast Florida throughout regions to the south. At the northern end of its range it is a 1- to 2-foot-tall ground cover, but in south Florida it may reach 10 feet. This shrub has decidedly wrinkled, deep green leaves.

Softleaf coffee (*P. sulzneri*) occurs in south and south-central Florida hammocks, usually as a somewhat lanky, 4- to 6-foot-tall shrub. The leaves are thin and grayish green with a velvety sheen. They are only slightly wrinkled. Softleaf coffee produces great amounts of bright red fruit—more than the other two species.

White indigo-berry (*Randia aculeata*) is a somewhat thorny, evergreen, 6- to 10-foot-tall shrub native to coastal woodlands in south and south-central Florida. The wood of this shrub is extremely dense, and the stout branches provide some cover for nesting birds. The leaves are small and nearly round. Fragrant white flowers bloom mostly in late spring to early summer. This species is dioecious. Round, 1/3-inch fruits ripen in late fall and winter. The bright white skins surround a deep purple flesh. White indigo-berry is an attractive, adaptable, and useful shrub for landscapes that don't receive frequent winter freezes.

Rutaceae (Citrus family)

Although citrus is not native to Florida, several genera of trees within this family are, and they are useful to wildlife. Members of this family have leaves with glands rich in aromatic oils. These oils are especially noticeable when the leaves are crushed or bruised. Most also have branches that are armed with spines or curved thorns. These are excellent cover trees for nesting birds and other wildlife. All species serve as the larval food plant for the giant swallowtail butterfly, and those that occur in the northern Florida Keys likely are used by the endangered Schaus' swallowtail butterfly.

swallowtail butterfly, and those that occur in the northern Florida Keys likely are used by the endangered Schaus' swallowtail butterfly.

Balsam torchwood (*Amyris balsamifera*) is a rare, 20-foot-tall, evergreen shrub native to hammocks of extreme south Florida. Leaflets often are composed of five, sometimes three, sharply pointed, oval leaves. The branches are thin and without thorns or spines. It has a rather irregular and open crown that is of moderate value as wildlife cover. Many small, white, fragrant flowers in terminal clusters bloom in early spring and in fall. The 1/2-inch, deep purple, berrylike fruits ripen in large clusters two to three months later. These are eagerly eaten by birds and small mammals. Balsam torchwood will grow well in the shade of a woodland setting, but will tolerate more sun if planted in the open.

Torchwood (*A. elemifera*) is virtually identical to balsam torchwood (*A. balsamifera*) except the leaflets usually are in groups of three, and the fruits are slightly smaller (about 1/3 inch). It occurs more widely throughout south Florida and sporadically in coastal hab-bocks along the east coast as far north as Cape Canaveral.

PRICKLY-ASHES (*Zanthoxylum* spp.) are small dioecious trees armed with hooked spines. The leaves are leathery and composed of many leaflets. The small flowers are in short racemes and are very attractive to pollinating insects. The fruits are small capsules that eventually open, exposing the 1/8-inch-diameter, hard, shiny black seeds. The seeds have some food value to birds and small mammals, but members of this genus are mostly useful for nesting and escape cover. Four species occur in Florida. All of them are quite salt tolerant.

Hercules club/toothache tree (*Zanthoxylum clava-herculis*) is a 20- to 30-foot-tall, deciduous tree native to well-drained coastal and inland habitats throughout most of Florida, except the Keys. It has a short trunk and a rounded crown. Almost every part of this tree is armed with stout prickles. Indians and early settlers reportedly chewed the leaves to deaden the pain of their toothaches. The chewed leaves numb both the lips and gums. Historically, the bark also was widely collected for medicinal uses. Flowering occurs

in late spring; the seeds are ripe by fall. Hercules club will grow as an understory tree, but looks best when given an open sunny location.

Biscayne prickly ash (*Z. coriaceum*) is a very rare, 20-foot-tall, evergreen tree native to coastal hammocks in a few locations in extreme south Florida. In many respects, it resembles wild lime (*Z. fagara*) described next, but the compound leaves are composed of large (4- to 8-inch), oval leaflets. This is an attractive tree, but its use is limited to frost-free areas of the state.

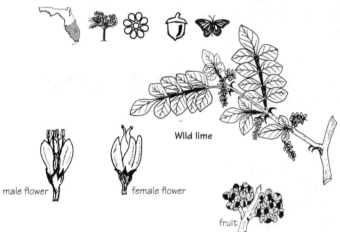

Wild lime

male flower

female flower

fruit

Wild lime (*Z. fagara*) is not a citrus-type lime, but a prickly ash, and it shares the characteristics of this genus. It is a small (20 to 25 feet), evergreen tree with a short trunk and thin, wide-spreading branches. The hooked thorns are small, but numerous, while the leaves are composed of 7 to 15 small, rounded leaflets. Wild lime occurs in coastal and interior woodlands throughout south and south-central Florida, and it will tolerate a variety of growing conditions. The greenish yellow flowers bloom in spring, and the seeds ripen by late summer or early fall.

Yellowheart/satinwood (*Z. flavum*) is another rare, evergreen tree found in only a few locations in the Florida Keys. It is normally about 15 feet in height with a broad, rounded crown. Unlike other members of this genus in Florida, it is not spiny. The wood of this tree has much commercial value, and it has been greatly exploited throughout its range in the Bahamas and West Indies. The compound leaves are composed of large (4- to 10-inch), oval leaflets. The flowers bloom in summer, and the seeds ripen by late fall. This beautiful small tree has much aesthetic appeal, but limited wildlife value.

Sapindaceae (Soapberry family)

This is a large tropical family with a few representatives in south Florida. Several non-native trees, including the litchi and logan, are greatly valued for their fruit and are grown commercially. Some native species, such as the soapberry (*Sapindus* spp.), have only limited wildlife value and are not described here.

Inkwood (*Exothea paniculata*) is a 40-foot-tall, broad-crowned tree found in coastal hammocks of south Florida and along the eastern coast as far north as Cape Canaveral. The wood is extremely strong and heavy, and the bark is reddish and often separates into large scales. The compound evergreen leaves normally are composed of four elliptical leaflets. These are a deep shiny green and occur mostly at the stem tips. Inkwood is dioecious. Small (1/4-inch-long), fragrant white flowers occur in loose clusters at the branch tips in late winter to spring. Numerous reddish purple, round fruits, 1/2 inch in diameter, ripen in midsummer. These are very attractive to birds and small mammals. Inkwood is an excellent food and cover tree for wildlife and has many aesthetic qualities besides. It is shade and salt tolerant and does best in alkaline soils with moderate drainage.

White ironwood (*Hypelate trifoliata*) is a rather rare, 30-foot-tall tree found in subtropical south Florida in both hammocks and pinelands. As its common name indicates, the wood is light in color, but dense and hard. It is a broad-crowned tree. The evergreen leaves are deep green, leathery, oval-shaped, and composed of three leaflets. Small (1/8-inch-long), white flowers are produced in clusters at the branch tips during early summer. Numerous sweet, black fruits, 1/3 to 1/2 inch in size, ripen by fall and are quickly eaten by birds and small mammals. Unlike inkberry, white ironwood is monoecious and produces fruit on each plant. This is a valuable wildlife tree and should be more commonly used in landscapes within its restricted range in Florida.

Sapotaceae (Sapote family)

Members of this medium-sized family occur primarily in tropical and subtropical regions of the world. All are either trees or shrubs with simple, leathery leaves, small, whitish flowers produced in small clusters along the stems at the leaf junctions, and rounded or egg-shaped fruits. Most species have a milky sap. Chicle, used to make chewing gum, is derived from the sap of the non-native sapodilla tree; and gutta-percha, an inelastic rubber used to make shoe soles and machine belts, is derived from other species of this family. Five genera native to Florida are good wildlife plants.

BUMELIAS (*Bumelia* spp.) are known sometimes as buckthorns, but should not be confused with buckthorns in the Rhamnaceae family. Bumelias are small trees or shrubs with dense, strong wood and often have thorns or thorny spurs along their branches. They are found throughout Florida in a wide variety of habitats. Their strong, dense, thorny branches produce good cover for wildlife, and their small, sweet, blackish fruits are an excellent food source for many songbirds and other wildlife. This is a confusing group for plant taxonomists. For this discussion, I will include seven species that generally are recognized as distinct.

Alachua buckthorn (*Bumelia anomala*) is a little known and poorly described shrubby tree that occurs around the Gainesville area and a few other hammocks in northeast and north-central Florida. The undersides of the oval, deciduous leaves are silvery pubescent. Branches are armed by thin thorns which eventually develop into short spur shoots. Alachua buckthorn grows naturally in moderate shade and soil moisture and in soils that are slightly alkaline. This seemingly rare tree grows to about 9 feet tall. Flowering occurs in the spring, and the 2/3-inch-long fruits ripen by late summer.

Saffron plum (*B. celastrina*) is a 20-foot-tall, evergreen tree native to the southern half of Florida. Its short trunk has a checkered and deeply fissured bark, and its crown is dense and rounded. Branches are slender and spreading and armed with short, rigid spines. All of the above characteristics make this plant excellent at providing wildlife cover. Highly aromatic flowers bloom in the spring and fall, attracting many insect pollinators. The 3/4-inch fruits ripen in summer and winter, and provide large amounts of wildlife food. Saffron plum is salt tolerant and adaptable to soil and light conditions. It is one of south Florida's best small trees for wildlife landscapes.

Wooly buckthorn/gum bumelia (*B. lanuginosa*) is an irregularly shaped, deciduous, shrubby tree that may reach 30 feet in height. Most common in sandy upland woodlands, it occurs in north and north-central Florida in a variety of inland and near-coastal habitats. The undersides of the oval-shaped leaves are covered with coppery-colored wool. The dark outer bark is deeply furrowed. Branches are thin and spreading, but rather open and not offering as much cover value as saffron plum. They also are only sparsely thorny. Wooly buckthorn produces large numbers of sweet, 2/5-inch-long fruit in the fall. This is a drought-tolerant species that also will tolerate medium shade.

Buckthorn bumelia (*B. lycioides*) is a shrubby, deciduous tree that may reach 30 feet in height. It occurs in moist soil habitats in limited areas of north Florida, and it is rare throughout its Florida range. This is a rather narrow-crowned species and the branches often are short and flexible. They are also often armed with short, stout thorns. The elliptical leaves are pointed and without pubescence. Flowering occurs in late spring, and the 2/3-inch fruits ripen by fall.

Smooth buckthorn (*B. reclinata*) is a deciduous, multi-stemmed shrub to about 15 feet in height, native to woodland areas of north and central Florida. It often occurs also in alkaline soils. Physical characteristics of this species are quite variable. Normally, the stems are crooked and thorny, and the leaves are oval to elliptical. The thin stems and rather open branching patterns create only moderate wildlife cover. Many white flowers bloom in the spring and produce large numbers of sweet, 1/3-inch fruits in the fall.

Rusty bumelia (*B. rufotomentosa*) is a low-growing shrub that rarely exceeds 1 foot in height. It frequently forms colonies by underground runners, thereby creating an excellent ground cover. Although the rounded to elliptical leaves generally are smooth, new stems are covered by a dense, rusty-colored pubescence. Stems also have short thorns.

Greenish white flowers produce 2/3-inch-long fruits by fall. Rusty bumelia inhabits sunny, well-drained areas of north and central Florida.

Silver buckthorn/tough bumelia (*B. tenax*) is an irregular, deciduous shrub or small (20-foot-tall) tree native to coastal and interior scrublands throughout Florida, except the Panhandle. This is another bumelia with greatly varying characteristics. Most specimens have stout, crooked branches with some thorns and numerous thorny spur shoots. Dense, rusty pubescence covers the new growth and the undersides of the leaves of many specimens. Tree forms of this plant provide excellent wildlife cover and are similar in many respects to saffron plum. Shrubby forms can be used to create thickets. Flowering occurs in late spring, and the 1/2-inch-long fruits ripen by fall. This bumelia requires good drainage and plenty of sunlight.

Thorne's bumelia (*B. thornei*) is a rare, deciduous shrub that rarely exceeds 15 feet in height. Found only in a small region of southern Georgia and in neighboring Jackson County, Florida, this is a poorly described and little known member of the bumelia genus. It occurs in low woodland areas that occasionally flood for short periods. Thorne's bumelia is rather spindly with few branches and many thorns and thorny spur shoots. Its leaves are glossy green and elliptical in shape. This shrub provides only marginal cover value to wildlife, and its restricted range and growing requirements limit its usefulness in the landscape. The blackish, 1/2-inch-long fruits provide food for birds and other wildlife, however.

Satinleaf (*Chrysophyllum oliviforme*) is an evergreen, 30-foot-tall, shrubby tree of south Florida woodlands. It has an upright, reddish trunk and slender, arching branches, which do not provide much cover or nest support. Most distinctive about this species is its oval leaves, which are deep green on top and covered by a dense felt of copper hairs beneath. Small, aromatic flowers are produced nearly year-round. The purple, 3/4-inch, plum-shaped fruits develop slowly. They are eagerly eaten by wildlife and are sometimes used to make jelly. Satinleaf is tolerant of a variety of growing conditions, but is not very tolerant of freezing temperatures.

Willow bustic (*Dipholis salicifolia*) is a 30-foot-tall, evergreen tree native to south Florida hammock woodlands and is closely related to the bumelias. It has an upright, narrow crown, and the branches are rather slender and arching. The willowlike leaves tend to hang downward from the stems, and the overall nature of this species makes it only moderately good at providing hiding cover and poor for nesting cover. Many small white flowers bloom for a period between February and May. The 1/4-inch, purplish black fruits ripen in summer. Willow bustic is tolerant of a variety of growing conditions, including some tolerance of freezing temperatures and moderate tolerance of salt.

Wild dilly (*Manilkara bahamensis*) is a 30-foot-tall, evergreen, shrubby tree native to coastal scrubs and hammocks in extreme south Florida. Characterized by its short, knotted trunk and wide, spreading crown, the deep green leaves are oval-shaped and leathery and grow in clusters at the ends of the stems. New growth is covered with reddish hairs. Wild dilly often grows as a dense, rounded shrub, and in this form it provides good wildlife hiding cover. The thin branches do not create good nesting conditions, however. Flowers are produced in loose clusters at the leaf axils during the spring and fall months. They attract bees. The 1- to 1 1/2-inch, brown, rounded, rough-skinned fruits ripen several months after the flowers bloom. The thick, spongy flesh is mostly of interest to small and medium-sized mammals.

Mastic/jungle plum (*Mastichodendron foetidissimum*) is a broad-crowned, evergreen tree, native to south Florida hammocks, that may reach 60 feet in height. It has some cold tolerance and occurs in coastal woodlands as far north as Cape Canaveral on the east coast. The broad, oval leaves are yellowish green with wavy margins and are clustered at the branch tips. Both the leaves and bark have a strong, fetid odor. Mastic provides good hiding cover, but only moderate nesting cover because most of the branches are long and thin. Light yellow, fragrant flowers bloom mostly in midsummer and attract many pollinating insects. Large numbers of yellow, 1/2-inch-long "plums" ripen from February to March. They are eaten and dispersed by a variety of wildlife.

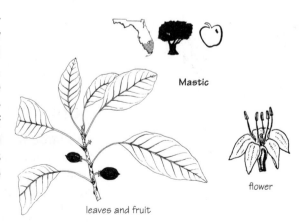

Mastic

leaves and fruit

flower

Simaroubaceae (Bitterbark family)

This is a small family of tropical trees and shrubs. Members are characterized by chemicals in their bark that are bitter to the taste. The bark of some species are used to make fever tonics. Leaves of most species are compound and featherlike in appearance. Two species, both of them dioecious and native to south Florida, have wildlife value.

Bitterbush (*Picramnia pentandra*) is a shrubby tree (usually about 10 feet in height) that occurs in coastal hammocks in south Florida, but not naturally in the Keys. It is a slender species and provides limited cover. Flowering is variable, but mostly occurs in summer. Although the flowers are inconspicuous, they are fragrant and attract bees and other insects. On the female plants, drooping, grapelike clusters of 1/2-inch fruits ripen from reddish to black by late fall. The fruits are eaten mostly by birds. Bitterbush is quite salt tolerant and will grow in a variety of conditions, including shade.

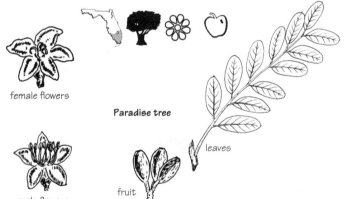

female flowers

Paradise tree

leaves

male flowers

fruit

Paradise tree (*Simarouba glauca*) is a rather common inhabitant of well-drained hammocks in south Florida, occurring in coastal hammocks as far north as Cape Canaveral. It is a slender, open-crowned tree with reddish brown and gray bark that may reach 50 feet in height, although it is a rather slow grower. New growth is reddish, adding to the aesthetic appeal of this tree. Terminal clusters of light yellow flowers bloom mostly in early spring, and the reddish purple, 3/4-inch fruits ripen a few months later on the female trees. They are sweet and eagerly sought after by birds and other wildlife. This tree should be grown in sunny upland locations within its range. It has good salt tolerance.

Solanaceae (Nightshade family)

This large family is composed of mostly herbaceous plants and contains some important food plants, including potatoes, eggplants, tomatoes, peppers, and ground cherries (tomatillos). Many species also are poisonous or contain powerful alkaloids that have medicinal uses in controlled amounts. These include the deadly nightshade (*Atropa* spp.), foxglove (*Digitalis* spp.), and angel's trumpet (*Datura* spp.). Two genera of native night-shades become woody and have wildlife value, primarily as food plants.

Christmas berry (*Lycium carolinianum*) is an unusual evergreen shrub that is native to coastal hammocks and marshes throughout Florida. Average mature height is about 10 feet. The gray-colored branches are slender and gnarled, frequently with occasional thorns. The leaves are succulent and needlelike. They often are shed for brief periods if the plant undergoes drought stress. Flowering occurs mostly in the fall, although a few flowers may be present throughout the year. Flowers are a beautiful light blue. These are followed by 1/3-inch, bright red, egg-shaped fruits that ripen mostly in early winter—hence, its common name. Christmas berry is an interesting accent plant that is adaptable to most home landscapes. It provides little cover, but birds eagerly devour the fruit.

NIGHTSHADES (*Solanum* spp.) are the largest genus in this family and contain many common weedy herbs. Three species of native woody nightshades are found in Florida. These generally occur as weakly branched, evergreen shrubs with simple, leathery leaves. The fruits are berrylike and, much like tomatoes, they contain many small seeds within the fleshy pulp. The fruits are designed to be eaten by birds, and the seeds are widely dispersed in their droppings. They have very limited use, however, as cover plants.

Bahama nightshade (*Solanum bahamense*) is a low shrub (rarely taller than 6 feet) native to coastal thickets in extreme south Florida. It is a species primarily of disturbed edges, but is adaptable to a variety of habitats within its limited geographic range. The leaves are rough textured, and the branches often are armed with spines. The purple flowers and the 1/3-inch, brilliant red fruits are produced throughout the year.

Potato tree (*S. donianum*) is a 5-foot-tall shrub native to disturbed edge habitats of extreme south Florida. White flowers are produced in clusters at the tips of the branches throughout the year. The 1/3-inch-long, bright red fruits are available nearly year-round.

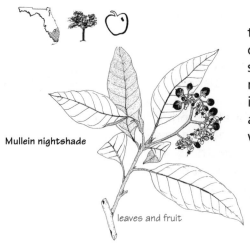

Mullein nightshade

flower

leaves and fruit

Mullein nightshade (*S. erianthum*) is an evergreen shrub or small tree that may reach 15 feet in height. It is native to disturbed habitats and coastal hammocks in central and south Florida. Its large, wooly leaves are similar in appearance to mullein (a common roadside weed)—hence, its name. Clusters of white flowers are produced year-round, as are the 1/3-inch, yellow fruits. Mullein nightshade eventually forms a rather flat crown and stout, spreading branches. Therefore, it provides a limited amount of wildlife cover.

Taxaceae (Yew family)

Yews are an ancient group of dioecious, evergreen trees and shrubs with needlelike leaves, confined primarily to northern climates. Two very rare species, however, are confined to Florida along the lower slopes of the deep wooded ravines of the Apalachicola River—a system that preserves a climate that prevailed in much of northern Florida during the last Ice Age. One of these, the Florida torreya (*Torreya taxifolia*) provides some wildlife cover, but little food value and is not discussed further. The other member is below.

Florida yew (*Taxus floridana*) is a shrub that may reach about 20 feet in height, but often is smaller. Like all yews, the needles are flat and flexible and the branches are numerous. These characteristics give it excellent value as wildlife cover. Fruiting cones are produced in late winter and the fruits ripen on female plants by fall. Fruits consist of a hard seed surrounded by a juicy, bright red aril. Birds especially are attracted to these fruits, and the seeds are dispersed in their droppings. Florida yew is a beautiful, aromatic shrub that has great landscape value. Its sensitivity to environmental conditions, however, restricts its use primarily to north Florida in locations that are relatively cool, moist, and partly shady.

Taxodiaceae (Bald Cypress family)

Cypresses (*Taxodium* spp.) are the signature trees of southern forested wetlands. Tall and picturesque, they dominate the ecosystem and play a vital role in the way it functions. Cypress also are adaptable to home landscapes, once established, and do not require wetland conditions to thrive. Bald cypress are large, long-lived, deciduous trees with broad trunks and scaly, reddish brown bark. They have a rather pyramidal shape when young, but older trees acquire a flattened crown. The broad branches provide homesites for many species of wildlife. Cypresses are dioecious. The cones produced on female trees provide seeds that are eaten by some birds and small mammals. Good seed production occurs only every three or four years, however. Although some taxonomists consider all cypresses in Florida to be varieties of the bald cypress, recent research and differences in characteristics indicate that the two forms are distinct. Therefore, I have split them.

Pond cypress (*Taxodium ascendens*) is characterized by leaves that are nearly needlelike and that extend upward from the branches. This gives pond cypress a very distinctive appearance, very much unlike the bald cypress. Pond cypresses also tend to occupy different habitats. Under natural conditions, they are found primarily in wet depressions adjacent to lakes, ponds, and other still waters. They are well-adapted to nonmoving water where depths of 4 to 6 feet may occur for extended periods, and they will grow on saturated shallow soils over limestone. In such shallow soils, they often are stunted and twisted. Pond cypress is not the best cypress for typical home landscapes, but it is preferred for use in and around the edges of retention ponds, lakes, and other wet areas where water stands for long periods.

Bald cypress (*T. distichum*) is characterized by short, feathery leaves. In other physical respects it looks much like the pond cypress. Bald cypress, however, normally grows near moving water, especially along the low banks of streams and sloughs and in the floodplains and backwaters of seasonally flooded areas. Although it may grow around ponds and lakes, it

Bald cypress

leaves with female cones

male cones

does best on shallow banks and not in the standing water. Bald cypress also is the best choice for home landscaping in a typical yard where it can be established.

Theophrastaceae (Joewood family)

This is a small family restricted to the American tropics and Hawaii. Although some members of the family are occasionally planted as ornamentals, most are rarely used and are of little importance commercially. One species in this family occurs naturally in south Florida.

Joewood (*Jacquinia keyensis*) is a shrubby tree that may reach 20 feet in height. It occurs in coastal hammocks and is therefore quite tolerant of salt and droughty soils. Joewood is an attractive landscape plant. The short, thick trunk is smooth and gray. Its many branches form a wide crown, and the evergreen, leathery, paddle-shaped leaves are concentrated near the branch tips. These features make it a useful cover tree both for nesting and hiding. Many ivory-colored flowers are produced throughout the year in clusters at the branch tips. They are extremely fragrant and attract many pollinating insects. Several months later, the round, 1/3-inch, yellow to orangish fruits ripen. These are eaten by birds and other wildlife. Joewood has many fine qualities to recommend its use in south Florida landscapes, but it is difficult to propagate and is not widely available at this time. It also is quite slow growing and requires several years before it produces wildlife benefits.

Ulmaceae (Elm family)

The elms are a medium-sized family of trees and shrubs distributed mostly in temperate regions of the northern hemisphere. Four separate genera are native to Florida. Elms have simple, asymmetrical, oval leaves with toothed margins and pointed tips. Small, non-showy flowers are produced mostly in the spring. The fruits of this family are variable in nature and wildlife value. Most members, however, provide excellent nesting and hiding cover.

HACKBERRIES (*Celtis* spp.) are a widely distributed genus with temperate and tropical representatives. They generally are characterized by rapid growth, but they are short-lived. Fruits are a round, fleshy berry. These are produced in abundance and are a good wildlife food source. Four species occur in Florida, but two are exceptionally rare and are listed as endangered species. All are deciduous.

Iguana hackberry (*Celtis iguanaea*) is a spiny, 3- to 10-foot-tall shrub native to Mexico, Central America, and northern South America, but confined to two small, isolated populations in coastal hammocks in south Florida. Often it is sprawling in its growth habit and, as such, it provides excellent wildlife cover for those species that prefer thickets. The round, yellow fruits are 1/2 an inch in diameter and ripen in late summer. They are edible and were used by native Americans. They also attract wildlife. Iguana hackberry grows on old shell middens in its Florida locations. It is very tolerant of salt and alkaline soils—and would have landscape value if it were available in nurseries.

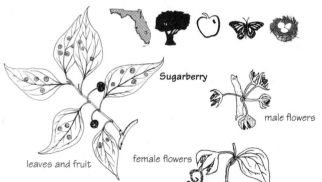

leaves and fruit

Sugarberry

male flowers

female flowers

Sugarberry (*C. laevigata*) is a large, 90-foot-tall tree common to moist woodland habitats throughout Florida, except the Keys. Characterized by its broad crown and thick, warty trunk, sugarberry soon becomes a dominant shade tree in areas where it is planted. Its large branches also provide homes for many species of wildlife. Flowering occurs in the spring, and large crops of 1/4-inch, plum-colored fruits ripen by early fall. Although the fruits have a rather thin flesh, they are eaten by many songbirds and other wildlife. Sugarberry will form root suckers and spread if allowed to. Young trees also will sprout from the large crops of bird-dispersed fruit. This is an adaptable tree for most landscape settings, but it is not salt tolerant.

Spiny hackberry (*C. pallida*) is another rare, spiny shrub confined to just two coastal shell mound sites in Florida. It is native also to the arid American southwest in habitats much different from those in Florida, so its habitat requirements here are not well known. A specimen in my yard, planted from south Texas seed, has grown well in alkaline soil next to my house. Spiny hackberry is a twisted, upright shrub that may reach 15 feet in height.

Short, straight spines near the leaf nodes improve its cover value for wildlife. Fruits are similar to those of iguana hackberry.

Georgia hackberry (*C. tenuifolia*) is a shrubby 20- to 30-foot-tall tree native to well-drained soils in north Florida. It normally has a rather irregular shape and an open crown with many short, slender branches. Its small stature and shape do not give it much cover value for wildlife, but the numerous 1/3-inch, reddish fruit are eaten by many birds and mammals in the fall. Georgia hackberry is adaptable to most home landscape situations, except areas near salt water, and could be used as an understory shrub for sunny or partly sunny locations.

Planer elm (*Planera aquatica*) is a rarely used, 50-foot-tall, deciduous tree native to wet soil habitats in north Florida. It is one of the few trees that will grow in shallow, permanently flooded areas, and it has much potential value for use in ponds and retention areas because of this. Planer elm is a slender tree with a short trunk, open crown, and thin, spreading branches. In older specimens, several trunks may form from basal sprouts. The trunks are scaly with long sections of the grayish outer bark flaking away and revealing a reddish inner bark. Planer elm has only modest value as wildlife cover, but the soft, 1/2-inch, burrlike fruits are an important food source for waterfowl and other wildlife. Flowering occurs in February and the soft seeds ripen by mid-March.

West Indian trema (*Trema lamarckianum*) is a 20-foot-tall, shrubby tree native to disturbed habitats in extreme south Florida. Young specimens are rather dense, but they develop a more open growth habit as they mature. Therefore, they have only limited value for wildlife cover. Large amounts of 1/8-inch, round, pink fruits are eagerly eaten by birds and other wildlife, and fruiting occurs nearly year-round. This "weedy", short-lived shrub requires a sunny location, but is adaptable to most growing conditions and is salt tolerant.

Florida trema (*Trema micrantha*) is a 30- to 40-foot-tall, evergreen tree native to open, disturbed areas of south and central Florida. It has larger leaves than West Indian trema and orange fruit. In other respects it differs little from it.

ELMS (*Ulmus* spp.) are widely used shade trees throughout their range in temperate regions of the northern hemisphere. Their relatively rapid growth, tall, straight trunks, and spreading crowns give them great ornamental value. Their numerous branches also provide a great many sites for nesting birds. Elms are deciduous and most common to fertile, moist soil habitats. They are not salt tolerant, but they are adaptable to many growing conditions. In most native species, flowering occurs in the spring before leaf-out, and the small, dry, winged seeds ripen within a few months. Good seed production generally occurs only every two to three years. The seeds are eaten by some birds and mammals, but they normally are not an important food source. Seeds of the spring-fruiting species tend to be used more, because they ripen at a time when other foods are scarce. Four species occur in Florida, although only two are widely distributed.

Winged elm (*Ulmus alata*) is a large (to 100 feet), distinctive tree native to upland woodland habitats in north and central Florida. Named for the corky wings that form on its limbs and trunk, this is one tree that is nearly as attractive in the winter without leaves as it is during the rest of the year. Winged elms have small leaves that turn yellow in the fall. Flowering occurs in late winter, and the 1/4-inch seeds ripen by late March. This drought-tolerant tree has a wide range of landscape uses within its natural range.

American elm (*U. americana*) is a large (about 70 feet) tree native to moist hardwood forest habitats in north and central Florida. This species has been devastated by Dutch elm disease in northern states, but to date this disease has not been a major problem in Florida. Two subspecies occur here: *U. a. americana* is typical of the species found throughout eastern North America, while *U. a. floridana*, which differs slightly in the tooth pattern along the leaf margins, is the type most commonly found in Florida. These "Florida elms" may be less sensitive to Dutch elm disease than the

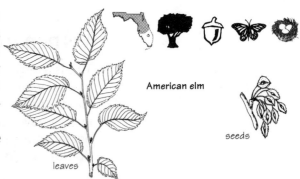

American elm

leaves

seeds

"American elm", but the data to show this is still lacking. Although fast-growing, this elm may live for hundreds of years. The leaves turn a rich yellow in the fall. Flowering occurs in the early spring and the 1/3-inch seeds ripen about one month later.

Cedar elm (*U. crassifolia*) is a medium-sized tree (to about 60 feet) native to moist woodland areas in widely scattered locations in north and central Florida. Its distribution here indicates that it prefers soils over limestone outcrops, and best growth likely will occur when it is planted in alkaline soils. Cedar elm often has corky wings along its branches, but this character is not as pronounced as it is in the winged elm. The trees have a distinct, irregular shape with drooping branches and a rather narrow crown. Leaves are small, like winged elm, but they are more oval in shape and have no sharp pointed tip. Cedar elm leaves are also rough on the upper surface. Cedar elm bears flowers and fruits in the fall. The seeds are about 1/3 inch in diameter. Leaves turn a yellowish brown in autumn.

Slippery elm (*U. rubra*) is a 60-foot-tall tree common in northern forests, but native in Florida only to the central and western Panhandle in fertile, moist woodland soils. This tree has a rounded crown and stout, spreading branches. The large leaves, which turn yellow in autumn, are rough on the upper surface. Its common name comes from the sticky slime in the inner bark that was once used to treat fevers and inflammations. Flowering occurs in the early spring, and the 1/2-inch, circular seeds ripen about a month later. This is a relatively long-lived elm, but its use in the landscape should be restricted to north Florida.

Verbenaceae (Verbena family)

This is a large, mostly tropical family that includes many species cultivated for their ornamental value. All woody species native to Florida are shrubs or shrubby trees. Most have leaves that contain glands with aromatic oils, and many of these are used in potpourris and to flavor teas and foods. Many also have showy, aromatic blooms that are excellent nectar sources for butterflies and other pollinating insects. As a rule, the native verbenas do not provide much cover value to nesting wildlife, but they have moderate value as hiding cover when they are planted in groupings. The species included in this discussion provide fruits that are eaten mostly by birds.

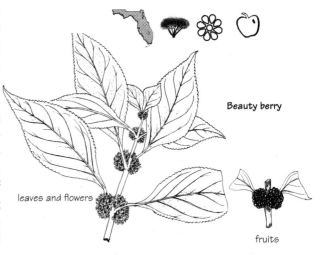

Beauty berry (*Callicarpa americana*) is a 6-foot-tall, deciduous shrub native to a wide variety of upland habitats throughout Florida. This is one of the most adaptable native shrubs, thriving in a wide variety of soil and moisture conditions and from full sun to shade. It is not tolerant of salt, however, and its best growth generally occurs in partly sunny locations. Beauty berry has numerous slender, wide-spreading branches and large, rough, oval leaves with toothed margins. Clusters of small pinkish flowers bloom along the stems at the leaf nodes in late spring. Unlike other members of this family, they do not seem attractive to butterflies and are pollinated mostly by bees. Numerous magenta-colored berries, 1/8 of an inch in diameter, ripen along the stems in the fall. This is the prettiest feature of this shrub, and the fruits may remain until late winter if they are not first eaten by birds. Beauty berry tolerates regular pruning, but is best used in areas where its arching branches have room to spread. A white-fruited form also is available in nurseries.

Beauty berry

leaves and flowers

fruits

Fiddlewood (*Citharexylum fruticosum*) is a shrubby, 25-foot-tall tree native to coastal hammocks in south-central Florida and coastal hammocks and pinelands throughout the southern regions of the state. The many thin branches, square twigs, and opposite, elliptical leaves with orangish veins are distinctive. An evergreen, fiddlewood sheds most of its leaves in late winter as its new leaves appear. Long racemes of white flowers bloom mostly in May and June, but some flowering occurs at other times. The flowers are extremely fragrant. Because this shrub is dioecious, the round, 1/3-inch, reddish brown, sticky fruits occur only on female plants. Large numbers of them ripen in the late fall. Fiddlewood is very salt tolerant and seems to grow best in sunny, moist locations.

Golden dewdrop (*Duranta repens*) is a 15-foot-tall, evergreen shrub widely planted in south-central and south Florida landscapes. Although there is some dispute as to whether it is truly native to the Florida Keys or whether it was introduced from nearby islands or Central America, I'm including it here. This is a broad-spreading shrub with thin branches

that cascade out from the main stem. Branches often are slightly spiny, and the oval leaves are one to three inches long and deep green. Flowers are produced year-round in racemes that often are 5 to 6 inches long. Usually, the star-shaped flowers are light lavender in color with dark lavender lines, but a white form also occurs. These flowers are followed several months later by 1/3-inch, golden yellow fruits that are poisonous to people but attractive to birds. Golden dewdrop is an adaptable shrub, has tolerance to salt spray, and will thrive in a wide variety of growing conditions.

LANTANAS (*Lantana* spp.) are widely occurring, evergreen shrubs in Florida, easily recognized for their attractive flower clusters. Often used for their ornamental value or for their attractiveness to butterflies, lantanas also produce large amounts of small fruits that attract birds. Two species are generally recognized as Florida natives. A third species, **common lantana** (*Lantana camara*), is a commonly occurring shrub along roadsides and other disturbed areas, but is not usually considered to be native.

Pineland lantana (*L. depressa*) is a low-growing ground cover shrub native to the pine rockland habitats of south Florida. This lantana is not nearly as adaptable as common lantana and prefers sunny locations with moist, sandy soils. It is not exceptionally drought tolerant and is not tolerant of salt. Pineland lantana has showy clusters of lemon-yellow flowers nearly year-round, followed by clusters of 1/8-inch fruits.

Wild sage (*L. involucrata*) is an upright, narrow-crowned shrub that may reach 5 feet in height. It is native to coastal hammock edges in south and south-central Florida. The small, rounded leaves are densely covered with aromatic oil glands, and the foliage, when crushed, smells much like sage. Small clusters of tiny white flowers bloom year-round. The 1/8-inch fruits are magenta in color. Wild sage is most adaptable to coastal landscapes in sunny locations.

Zygophyllaceae (Lignum vitae family)

This is a medium-sized family that is widely distributed in the tropics and subtropics in both arid and tropical habitats. Some members produce valuable timber, but generally the family has little economic use and has not been widely used in landscapes. One species occurs in Florida.

Lignum vitae (*Guaiacum sanctum*) is an exceptionally slow-growing, evergreen tree native to hammock woodlands of extreme south Florida. Demand for its valuable wood and its slow growth rate have made it far less common than it once was, and it is now listed as an endangered species. Lignum vitae, or tree of life as the name translates, is one of Florida's most exceptional native trees. Rarely reaching 20 feet in height, it forms a large trunk and spreading branches that bend and curve much like those of a live oak. The leaves are opposite along the gray-white stems and are composed of glossy, dark green leaflets, six to eight in number. The dense, rich foliage is attractive and provides good cover. The flowers also are exceptional—they are star-shaped and deep blue in color. Flowering occurs mostly in the spring. By fall, the five-angled, yellowish seed capsules ripen and split open, revealing the five 3/4-inch-long seeds inside, each with a fleshy red aril. These are attractive mostly to birds. Lignum vitae is adaptable to most conditions, including salt spray, and makes a beautiful and interesting addition to the landscape in the warmer regions of Florida.

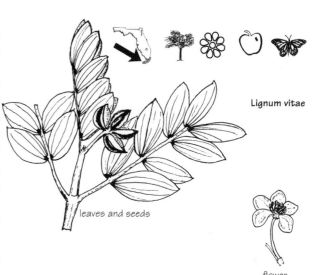

Lignum vitae

leaves and seeds

flower

Make a Difference! _____ FOUR

Perhaps our greatest opportunity to help wildlife is to improve habitat conditions around our homes and the areas where we live and work. As custodians of our own personal piece of the planet, we need to recognize ourselves as wildlife managers and to make active decisions for the benefit of those species that might live within our sphere of influence. Effective wildlife management does not occur by accident; it takes planning and consideration. It also tests our commitment and our creativity.

For those of us who enjoy gardening and marvel at the wondrous complexity of the natural world, there can be few efforts more rewarding than designing a landscape that produces wildlife. By expanding the diversity of wild creatures that reside around us, we enrich our lives and sew an even stronger thread within the great web of life.

Most developed landscapes produce far too few surprises. There is nothing really new to anticipate around the corner of the street or the change in season in most places where we live. We have come to expect sameness, and we have accepted it far too long. The forces of nature do not stop at the edge of town. An environmental ethic must replace the commonly held belief that our yards are ours. We cannot afford to give up on urbanized areas because they are not "natural".

Diversity can replace sameness. Our concept of urban wildlife can embrace many more species than we normally consider. But this will be accomplished only when we become creative in our design and management of developed landscapes, and when we use a greater diversity of native plants than we currently do. Our hope is that this reference will help guide us towards this goal.

FIVE Selected Wildlife Landscape Plants by Region _____

The following are lists of some of the most useful native trees and shrubs for Florida wildlife landscaping. As in the text, the plants are arranged by their growth form (i.e., medium to large trees, small trees, and shrubs). Separate lists have been produced also for broad geographic regions of Florida so that you can focus on the plants that best fit the area where you live.

Common and scientific names are given, followed by a letter code that designates the season when the fruit ripens. Even a casual glance at this list reveals that most fruits ripen in summer and fall. This is especially true in the northern half of Florida. While some fall-bearing plants hold their uneaten fruit well into winter, others don't. Late winter and spring are problem months for supplying seeds, nuts, and soft fruits for wildlife, and it is these times when your creativity will be most challenged.

Lists such as these should be viewed *only* as a starting point for your own planning. It should *not* be inferred that these plants are necessarily superior to those that are not listed. Each landscape setting is unique, as are the goals and tastes of the landscaper. These lists are not "complete". Do not use them to avoid careful reference to the text or the necessary exercize of planning.

These lists are biased strongly to favor songbirds over mammals and other wildlife. There also is a bias for food production instead of cover. Your needs may require you to slant your biases differently.

NORTH FLORIDA SPECIES

Large Trees

American holly (*Ilex opaca*) F
Southern red cedar (*Juniperus silicicola*) F
American beech (*Fagus grandifolia*) F
Live oak (*Quercus virginiana*) F
Laurel oak (*Quercus laurifolia*) F
Red bay (*Persea borbonia*) Su/F
Red mulberry (*Morus rubra*) Su
Water tupelo (*Nyssa aquatica*) F
Black gum (*Nyssa sylvatica*) F
Cabbage palm (*Sabal palmetto*) F
Slash pine (*Pinus elliottii*) Su/F
Longleaf pine (*Pinus palutris*) Su/F
Black cherry (*Prunus serotina*) Su
Bald cypress (*Taxodium distichum*) F
Sugarberry (*Celtis laevigata*) Su/F

Small Trees

Dahoon holly (*Ilex cassine*) F
Yaupon (*Ilex vomitoria*) F
Flowering dogwood (*Cornus florida*) F
Swamp dogwood (*Cornus foemina*) F
Sparkleberry (*Vaccinium arboreum*) F
Downy serviceberry (*Amelanchier arborea*) Su
Mayhaw (*Crataegus aestivalis*) Su
Green haw (*Crataegus viridis*) F
Southern crabapple (*Malus angustifolius*) F
Chickasaw plum (*Prunus angustifolius*) Su
Flatwoods plum (*Prunus umbellata*) Su

Shrubs

Walter viburnum (*Viburnum obovatum*) F
Highbush blueberry (*Vaccinium corymbosum*) Su
Southern wax myrtle (*Myrica cerifera*) F
Flatwoods privet (*Forestiera ligustrina*) Su
Saw palmetto (*Serenoa repens*) Su
Beauty berry (*Callicarpa americana*) F

CENTRAL FLORIDA SPECIES

Large Trees

American holly (*Ilex opaca*) F
Southern red cedar (*Juniperus silicicola*) F
Live oak (*Quercus virginiana*) F
Laurel oak (*Quercus laurifolia*) F
Red bay (*Persea borbonia*) Su/F
Red mulberry (*Morus rubra*) Su
Black gum (*Nyssa sylvatica*) F
Cabbage palm (*Sabal palmetto*) F
Slash pine (*Pinus elliottii*) Su/F
Longleaf pine (*Pinus palustris*) Su/F
Cherry laurel (*Prunus caroliniana*) F/W
Bald cypress (*Taxodium distichum*) F
Sugarberry (*Celtis laevigata*) Su/F

Small Trees

Dahoon holly (*Ilex cassine*) F
Yaupon (*Ilex vomitoria*) F
Flowering dogwood (*Cornus florida*) F
Swamp dogwood (*Cornus foemina*) F
Sparkleberry (*Vaccinium arboreum*) F
Simpson stopper (*Myrcianthes fragrans*) Su
Green haw (*Crataegus viridis*) F
Chickasaw plum (*Prunus angustifolia*) Su
Flatwoods plum (*Prunus umbellata*) Su

Shrubs

Walter viburnum (*Viburnum obovatum*) F
Highbush blueberry (*Vaccinium corymbosum*) Su

Southern wax myrtle (*Myrica cerifera*) F
Florida privet (*Forestiera segregata*) Sp/Su
Saw palmetto (*Serenoa repens*) Su
Beauty berry (*Callicarpa americana*) F

SOUTH FLORIDA SPECIES

Large Trees

Gumbo-limbo (*Bursera simaruba*) W
Red bay (*Persea borbonia*) Su/F
Strangler fig (*Ficus aurea*) Sp-W
Cabbage palm (*Sabal palmetto*) F
Slash pine (*Pinus elliottii* var. *densa*) Su/F
Mastic (*Mastichodendron foetidissimum*) Sp
Paradise tree (*Simarouba glauca*) Su
Bald cypress (*Taxodium distichum*) F
Sugarberry (*Celtis laevigata*) Su/F

Small Trees

Dahoon holly (*Ilex cassine*) F
all Stoppers (*Eugenia* spp.) various
Simpson stopper (*Myrcianthes fragrans*) Su
Blolly (*Guapira discolor*) Su/F
Pigeon plum (*Coccoloba diversifolia*) F
Sea grape (*Coccoloba uvifera*) F
Black ironwood (*Krugiodendron ferreum*) W
Darling plum (*Reynosia septentrionalis*) F
West Indian cherry (*Prunus myrtifolia*) Su
White ironwood (*Hypelate trifoliate*) F
Saffron plum (*Bumelia celastrina*) Su,W
Joewood (*Jacquinia keyensis*) Sp/W

Shrubs

Cat's claw (*Pithecelobium unguis-cati*) Su
Locust-berry (*Byrsonima lucida*) Su
Southern wax myrtle (*Myrica cerifera*) F

Florida privet (*Forestiera segregata*) Sp/Su
Saw palmetto (*Serenoa repens*) Su
Firebush (*Hamelia patens*) Su/F
White indigo-berry (*Randia aculeata*) F/W
Beauty berry (*Callicarpa americana*) F

GLOSSARY

Though I have used very few botanical terms in this book in an effort to make it easily readable for non-professionals, once in a while I have let some scientific language slip in. In case you need it, here is a short glossary.

acid—a pH of less than 7.0.

alkaline—a pH of greater than 7.0.

aril—fleshy material partially surrounding or covering a seed.

axil—the upper angle between a structure and the axis that bears it, such as the angle between a leaf and the stem bearing the leaf.

compound leaf—a leaf composed of two or more distinct leaflets.

deciduous—describing a plant that loses its leaves seasonally.

dioecious—describing a plant that has male and female flowers on different plants.

endemic—a species whose natural range is restricted to a very small geographic area.

geniculate—bent at abrupt angles, exhibiting a zig-zag pattern.

inflorescence—a cluster of flowers.

leaf node—site on the stem where the leaf attaches.

monoecious—describing a plant that has male and female flowers on the same plant.

pubescent—covered with short, soft "hairs".

raceme—a simple elongated inflorescence of flowers, each flower being attached by short stalks.

sucker—a secondary shoot arising from the root of the parent plant, which has the ability to develop into a separate mature plant.

umbel—an inflorescence of few to many flowers with each flower being attached by a stalk from a common point of attachment. Such inflorescences tend to look "flat".

INDEX ━━━━━━━━━━━━━━━━━━━━━